LIVING TRUSTS
for Everyone

Why a Will Is Not the Way
to Avoid Probate, Protect Heirs,
and Settle Estates

BY RONALD FARRINGTON SHARP

© 2010 Ronald Farrington Sharp

**ALLWORTH
PRESS**
NEW YORK

14   13   12   11   5   4   3   2

Published by Allworth Press
An imprint of Allworth Communications, Inc.
10 East 23rd Street, New York, NY 10010
Cover design by Esther Wu
Interior design by Esther Wu
Page composition/typography by Integra Software Services, Pvt., Ltd., Pondicherry, India

ISBN-13: 978-1-58115-674-4

Library of Congress Cataloging-in-Publication Data:
Sharp, Ronald Farrington.
Living trusts for everyone : why a will is not the way to avoid probate, protect heirs, and settle estates / by Ronald Farrington Sharp.
       p. cm.
Includes index.
ISBN 978-1-58115-674-4
1. Living trusts—United States.
2. Estate planning—United States.
I. Title.
KF734.S53 2010
346.7305'2—dc22   2009040383

This book is not intended as legal or tax advice since laws vary from jurisdiction to jurisdiction and change frequently, so if you have legal questions about your particular situation you should ask them of an attorney in your state.

Printed in the United States of America

CONTENTS

Preface

Much has been written about using the living trust to avoid probate. One would assume from the information out there that probate avoidance is the most important value of having a trust. But, for many people, there are far more important and even critical reasons to have a trust rather than a will.

There are four fundamental purposes and advantages of a trust.

The first is asset management. It could be a mistake to give certain beneficiaries a lump sum inheritance. They may be too young to properly manage money on their own, may be mentally incapable of managing it, or may not have enough maturity or good sense to be good money managers. Using a will to leave your assets to your young children may result in money going to someone too young to properly manage it.

Minors can inherit from their parents or others. Unless the inheritance is left to them in a trust, the money is kept for them by their guardian and conservator. Then, when they reach the "age of majority" (adulthood—usually eighteen), whatever is left of the money they inherit is turned over to them as a lump sum.

Even adult heirs may be incapable of managing money properly. Having their share in trust for them allows someone else to be sure it is properly invested and managed. Those who receive certain governmental benefits, including disabled heirs who need help with medical costs and rely on Medicaid, may be disqualified from receiving those benefits if they inherit too much that is not in the right sort of trust for them.

The second benefit is tax reduction. While the estate tax now hits fewer people than before due to the high threshold, a trust of one kind or another can either eliminate or greatly reduce estate and inheritance taxes. This purpose is considered by many nonexpert attorneys to be the only reason to have a trust—thus their oft-given yet erroneous advice: You don't have enough money to need a trust.

The third advantage is probate avoidance, which is a valuable benefit. The big lie put forth by some attorneys and bar associations is that probate is not that expensive and there is no good reason to try to avoid it. The truth is that probate is usually very expensive (because of attorney fees) and is in nearly all cases totally unnecessary if a properly prepared and funded living trust had been prepared. Attorneys who say a trust is not needed are either ignorant of the value of trusts or have a vested interest in seeing probate continue.

The fourth benefit is for those who wish to avoid a court-ordered conservatorship should they become so disabled as to be unable to manage their own affairs. If, for example, a person has dementia, the trust can have provisions that allow a successor trustee (the one who would take control at death) to take over financial management of the trust assets. This helps the person avoid the expense and embarrassment of court supervision.

There is also a grab bag of additional benefits, including privacy (probate is public record; trusts are most often not), low cost (there are no court costs, filing fees, or estate inventory fees on a trust at death), ease of administration, lower likelihood of someone contesting the estate, and elimination of the time delay caused by probate of a will.

I have also included in this volume a set of instructions for the family to follow at death. Most often, attorneys do not provide instructions and the family has no idea what to do when the trustmaker dies. So they go back to the attorney who prepared the trust and end up paying a lot of money to find out what to do. The fact is that a trustee does not need legal services to settle the trust since the things that need to be done are clerical, not legal, in nature. Why pay attorney rates for clerical work? The information in this section is invaluable and not available from most sources.

The information contained herein will benefit both those who do not have a trust as well as those who do. This is not a textbook or a comprehensive treatise on all the many kinds of trusts that can be done for various reasons, nor will you find out how to do your own trust. This is a book for the 95 percent of the population that has done no estate planning, so that they are informed and will not be misled by incorrect information pushed by those with vested interests in seeing the probate process continue.

Introduction

When I was in law school back in 1973, I took an introductory course on trusts and estates. Our class was visited by an old-time lawyer (probably about the age I am right now) who gave us what he considered practical and useful advice in starting out in the practice of law. I will paraphrase his advice as I remember it.

We were in one of the big lecture halls and he stood onstage at the podium, then began to pace much as I imagined he did while talking to a jury.

When you young people get done with law school and pass the bar, most of you will be going into private practice. You will meet a lot of people who want you to do their wills. A lot of them will be your own age. I am going to tell you how to make the most of this opportunity.

Now, you don't make much money on a will. In fact, you don't want to. Consider it a loss leader. The thing to do is do these wills real cheap. Word will get out and you will have a lot of wills to do. How you do it is important. First, when you write it up, be sure to put in that they want you to be the attorney who handles the estate—put it right in the will. Get some nice printed-up will paperwork with fancy lettering and your name and address printed on the envelope. Then, make sure that you have a Will File. Keep the original copy of the will and give the client a photocopy and a receipt for the original. Tell them this is normal procedure so the will is kept safe.

Now what will happen is that as the years go by your Will File gets bigger and bigger. Then, your clients start to die off. When they do, the family has to come to you because you have the will. Naturally, they expect that you will be the lawyer for the estate, since you are named in the will and have the original. So now, as you reach the last half of your practice, you have a built-in probate practice. Probate is very lucrative. This, ladies and gentlemen, is your retirement plan.

I thought then (and still do) that this was a very sleazy tactic—one that gives all lawyers a bad name. We have enough trouble with our public image as it is. Yet this practice is still going on and no one is the wiser. Clients are not getting the proper advice and planning they rely on, and lawyers are getting rich.

The fact is that in most all cases probate is not necessary and is easily avoided. If proper planning is done, there should be no legal fees at all after a person's death.

I have found that people are lost at sea when a person dies and seek help—usually from a lawyer. They are then charged hundreds of dollars an hour for many hours simply because only the lawyer knows what needs to be done at death, even if the deceased has made very careful plans to simplify the estate and keep it out of probate. So included as the last chapter is an actual set of step-by-step instructions—the secret is now out of what to do at death.

I wrote this book as a way of educating and helping people. This is not a textbook, nor does it cover in detail all the kinds of trusts available for those with complex estate plans. You won't find any forms in here to make your own trust. I hope that I have explained trusts in a simple and understandable way so you as the reader and potential client know as much about trusts as most of the lawyers out there.

DISCLAIMER:

This book is not intended as legal or tax advice since laws vary from jurisdiction to jurisdiction and change frequently, so if you have legal questions about your particular situation you should ask them of an attorney in your state.

CHAPTER ONE

Trusts and Wills Defined

Years ago I started doing revocable trusts as a way of keeping my clients out of probate. Now, after having done nearly four thousand trust-based estate plans, I can confidently assure you that a will is not the way to plan your estate.

Wills have to be probated.

Trusts don't.

Most people believe good estate planning is having a last will and testament made up by their local lawyer. Most people are wrong. The reason they believe wills are good is because they pay their lawyer, who tells them so. Of course, lawyers usually have a vested interest in seeing you go through probate. Much of the cost of probate is attorney fees. It is not, as they would have you believe, "court costs."

The actual cost of probate is unpredictable in most cases. It is usually based on the hourly rate of the lawyer—which may be hundreds of dollars per hour—multiplied by the total amount of time to complete the case. There can be a big incentive to "bill hours." Every telephone call, letter, meeting, and court appearance is recorded and billed. Since probate cases usually go on for one, two, or three years, the cost can be very high indeed. And attorney hourly rates vary widely. Hourly rates for probate work may run from $150 to $500 per hour, so it doesn't take long for the bill to get very large.

The family that hires the attorney rarely complains about the fees, thinking that there is nothing that can be done, and accepts whatever is billed to the estate. Here is a tip and something most people do not realize: Attorney fees are negotiable in most cases, and you can also, even in a probate case, ask the attorney to allow family members to do as much of the non-legal work as possible to keep the bill down. This is rarely done and no one has ever asked me to do this.

Probate is, for the most part, pretty simple stuff. Except in contested cases or where litigation is needed, the probate process consists of filing a series of fill-in-the-blank forms in the right sequence and timeframe. It is not unusual for a legal assistant or secretary to fill out the forms. The attorney involvement in the process is typically very minimal, even though the case is often billed as if the attorney was hands-on every step of the way. The point is that you are paying a lot of money for what amounts to clerical work.

It's not always billable hours. Certain states set the attorney fee portion of the probate cost as a percentage of the gross estate. This may actually be even more unfair than the hourly rate method. In California, for example, the following are the maximum rates that attorneys can charge for probate (and you can bet that nearly everybody is going to charge the maximum).

4 percent on the first $15,000
3 percent on the next $85,000
2 percent on the next $900,000
1 percent on the next $9 million
0.5 percent on the next $15 million

So a typical $500,000 estate would have attorney fees of $13,000—a lot of money. However, the executor (also called the personal representative) would be entitled to an additional $13,000 fee. So now we are up to $26,000 and have not included the cost of bonds, filing fees, and publication costs. This is, in my opinion, a very unfair way for costs to be assessed. It may take no more effort or time to probate a $150,000 estate than it does a $500,000 one, yet the fees are vastly different and not related to the effort expended or expertise needed. Most states have gotten away from the percentage fee because of this disparity, but an hourly rate may actually end up costing the estate more. Court costs are now being looked at as a source of revenue for the state. Florida is considering (if they haven't already done it by the time you read this) increasing the court filing fee for probate to $1,000 (and up to $2,000), up from the $280 currently charged. This is in addition, of course, to executor fees and attorney fees. Then there is the tax levied on the size of the probate case in some states. This is sometimes called an "inventory fee," and is a percentage of the total estate paid to the court or the county treasurer. Personally, whenever I write a check to the government I think of it as a tax by another name. None of these costs is incurred in independent trust administration.

The time involved is another big problem with probate. The probate case may have a minimum time that it must be 'open' to allow potential creditors of the deceased to present claims against the estate. Even in a simple one-asset estate, the case may have to stay open for a minimum of six months. But since there are no firm deadlines in probate, many attorneys put off closing it up and concentrate on their cases that do have deadlines, like court trials and real estate closings. The probate estate can be kept on the bottom of the pile. I have read that the average time to close a probate case is fifteen to eighteen months. This will vary state to state and attorney to attorney, with some estates being kept open for years.

So avoiding probate is a big deal, no matter what your law-yer tells you. And the living trust is the best way to do it.

According to the National Association of Estate Planning Councils, only about 5 percent of people with an estate have done any estate planning at all. And most of those have done a will rather than a trust. For those who die without a will, most folks rely on state law to determine what happens to their estate at death. A will may be better than nothing at all, but it pales in comparison to the value of a trust.

Before we go too far, let's define our terms. What exactly is the difference between a will and a trust?

WHAT IS A WILL?

A will is really just a written document telling who gets what part of your stuff at your death, when they get it, and who is in charge of getting the assets to the people who are supposed to get them. You can write your own will in your own handwriting (what lawyers call a holographic will) or it can be typed up, usually by a lawyer, and ceremonially witnessed and/or notarized. You can buy a will online or even get a fill-in-the-blank one at the office supply store. Some states even have a state-promulgated "statutory will," which is another fill-in-the-blank form. Wills are pretty easy to make and are usually less expensive to create than a trust. The big cost of a will comes later, when the probate fees are counted in.

The executor (also called the personal representative or sometimes the administrator) is the one who is in charge of seeing that these written instructions in the will are carried out under the supervision of the court.

The instructions in the will are really instructions to the probate court—who gets what when, and who's in charge. After your death, if there is anything left in your name to be probated, it is necessary to file the will in probate court because a court order is the only way your heirs can get your stuff turned over to them legally. There are a number of ways to avoid having things in your own name that have to be probated, such as giving everything away before you die or having everything in joint ownership, but these methods have problems of their own to be explained later in this book.

An example: I had a client who married a woman who owned a house in her name only. They lived in her house together for years, and he even signed on to the mortgage when it was refinanced. She then died suddenly. The house was in her name alone and his name was never added to the deed. My client was very upset when I explained that the house was not his until the probate court said so. His wife had made a will that left everything to him, but that was not in itself enough— which was a big surprise to him. He could not get full title to the house transferred to him until the probate court process was completed and all the expenses were paid. This case cost thousands of dollars in probate costs because of poor planning.

Another example: Dad dies, leaving no wife but three adult children. He has a house and some bank accounts and other investments. He has a will that says everything goes equally to his children. In order for those children to sell the house, they need to prove they own it. Unfortunately, the will in itself is not sufficient proof for a land title company or a real estate mortgage company that the house now belongs to the children— they want a court order that the will is valid and the property belongs to the children. The will has to be probated to get that order and clear the title.

Interestingly, in most states the will in the above example is totally useless and was a waste of money for Dad. The reason is that if a person dies without a will, then state law determines who are a person's heirs. These laws are called the laws of descent and distribution in case of intestacy (who gets what when somebody dies without a will). In the Dad-and-three-kids example, most state laws say that children whose parent dies without a spouse share his estate equally. A will adds nothing to that. The probate process is virtually identical with or without a will, so whoever charged Dad for that will did nothing for the money. Dad should have had a trust.

WHAT IS A TRUST?

A trust is also just a written document. It also says who gets what, when they get it, and who is in charge of seeing that that happens. The person in charge is the trustee. The difference is that a trust does not have to go through the probate court.

The reason a trust is not probated is that when a trust is signed, it becomes a legal entity that has the ability to own things. I often analogize it to the hardware store down the street. Smith's Hardware is a corporation. The corporation owns the building, the inventory, the delivery truck, the hardware bank account, the money in the cash register—all the hardware store assets. The Smiths own the corporation. If they die, the corporation is, in a sense, still alive and will keep selling hardware. New owners come in and take over the business operation.

A trust is similar. In a trust, the trust owners (the "grantors," "trustors," or "settlors") transfer their assets into the name of the trust. Let's call it "The Smith Trust." After they sign the trust document, The Smiths then "fund" the trust. In other words they transfer their assets into the trust name. This is done in a few ways, but typically real estate is deeded into the name of the trust by using a quit claim deed. Bank accounts may either be put into the name of The Smith Trust or may pay on death (POD) to the trust (kind of like a beneficiary designation). Life insurance is transferred by naming the trust as the beneficiary. Tax deferred accounts like IRAs and 401(k)s may have the trust as the primary or contingent beneficiary.

The idea is to have The Smith Trust own all the Smiths' assets. That way, at the death of the Smiths, there is nothing left in their individual names for the probate court to administer. The trust owns their stuff, but they own the trust. They die and the trust still owns their stuff, but the trust document then kicks in. The trust says who takes over at their death to carry out their instructions on who gets what and when.

The great thing is that there is no court order needed for the trustee to take over after the Smiths die. The trustee merely has to show proof that they are dead and show the trust to prove who is the trustee. Then, literally the day after they die, the trustee can begin carrying out their instructions on distributing the trust assets. How the trustee does all this is explained in simple language in the last chapter.

Now, of course, the trustee still has to do the normal things that need to be done when a person dies. The garage has to be cleaned out, the credit card bills and funeral and burial expenses paid, and the last year's income tax filed, but the trustee just goes ahead and does these things. No lawyer is needed and no legal or court fees are due.

People worry that a trust will tie up their property. Not true. In a revocable trust, the trust owners (grantors) have full rights to all trust assets during their lifetime. They can sell these, give them away, mortgage them, or even burn them up or gamble them away if they want without anyone's permission or any special paperwork. A trust is a death planning device and does not complicate the owner's life—if it is put together properly. Now the trustee is in a different position after the death or disability of the grantors. We call a trustee that name because this is someone the grantor picks who is trustworthy. Trustees have legal responsibilities to the trust beneficiaries. Trustees cannot, in most cases, change the terms of the trust in the way the grantors can. They can only follow the instructions of the grantors. And the trustee cannot do anything risky with the trust assets. State law requires a trustee to be very conservative in investing and dealing with trust assets. A trustee is called a "fiduciary" because they have a special responsibility to the beneficiaries to safeguard the trust assets for the benefit of the beneficiaries until all the trust assets are ultimately distributed as the grantors have instructed.

Your own lawyer may tell you that a simple will is all you need and that you do not have enough assets to consider a trust. Your lawyer is either lying to you or is ignorant of the facts about trusts. Many lawyers have been minimally trained in trust law and believe that the only reason to have a trust is for wealthy people to avoid estate taxes. Wrong.

The fact is that nearly everyone would be better off with a trust than with a will. In most cases the only person who benefits from your having a will instead of a trust is your lawyer. Attorney fees for making the will and probating the estate are a lawyer's bread and butter.

Of course, sometimes a lawyer can arrange it so a trust is no better or cheaper than a will. Some attorneys charge what they call a "settlement fee" to help the family wrap up the trust after death. This may be a percentage of the trust assets. The services provided by the lawyers are not, for the most part, legal services but they are charged for just as if they were. I will speak more to the issue of attorney fees and trust settlement later.

I have been talking so far about a simple trust for the normal family situation—what the IRS calls a revocable grantor trust, and which is often called a living trust. There are a lot of kinds of trusts with a lot of functions, including estate tax avoidance and charitable purposes, but most of the situations normal people find themselves in are easily handled using a simple revocable trust. In the next chapter I will explain who absolutely should have a trust and what it will do for them.

One more note: It is possible to put the provisions for a trust in the language of the last will and testament. A trust of this kind is called a testamentary trust. It may contain all the provisions of a stand-alone trust document and accomplish the same things. But because it is in a will, the trust is not created until probate is finished. It is then funded with some or all of the assets left after the probate process is completed and all the costs deducted.

Anyone with this type of trust is losing the major benefit of probate avoidance. This is not the type of trust you want. The testamentary trust is a great deal for the lawyer, since he gets paid for doing the trust as well as probating the estate. Good estate planners no longer use testamentary trusts. If one is recommended to you, be sure you ask why a revocable living trust is not being prepared instead.

CHAPTER TWO

You Must Have a Trust If ...

Having a trust is a nice thing for most people, and if they should not have one, the worst that can happen is that their estate gets probated, which takes a lot of time and costs the family a lot of money. A shame, but not the end of the world. For a lot of folks a trust is an absolute necessity to protect their family's financial future. If you are in any of the following situations, a trust is critical, and anyone who says you do not need one in any of these situations is flat-out wrong.

MINORS

If you do not have a trust and die while your children are still young, the inheritance will be given to them in a lump sum when they reach the "age of majority"—age eighteen in most states. In the meantime, the money is held in a court-supervised conservatorship account under the control of the minor's guardian or conservator. There are three things wrong with this.

First, in my experience, turning over a lump sum of cash to an eighteen-year-old is a bad idea. I have seen it happen, and time and again, the money is wasted. In fact, leaving a large amount of money to an eighteen-year-old is actually a disincentive to their education. The child has never had any significant amount of money before, does not know how to manage it, and might think that going to college is not necessary with "all that money" in the bank. Unfortunately, the money soon disappears through bad management, poor decisions, and excessive spending. I have seen a number of eighteen-year-olds inherit money that they no longer have at age nineteen or twenty. Then, when they do want to go to school, there is no way to pay for it.

The second problem is the court-supervised conservatorship. It sounds like a good idea to have a judge oversee the child's money, but in fact this can be a very complex and time-consuming process for the guardian who is acting as conservator of the money. Virtually every decision made by the conservator has to be passed by the judge. The money has to be put into restricted accounts over which the conservator has little investment control. In most jurisdictions, the conservator must prepare an annual accounting of income and expenses, prepare a written annual report, and appear in front of the judge for the judge's approval. Every year. True, we need oversight in some cases to be sure the conservator will not steal the money, but I find that the conservator is typically a grandparent, aunt, or uncle who would not steal from the child in a million years.

The third problem is that the guardian of the child is most often also the conservator of the money. Again, this seems logical, but I often have divorced parents tell me they want to be sure the other parent, the ex-spouse, does not end up in control of the child's money for one reason or another—usually because they do not trust the ex to use the money for the best interests of the child.

With a trust, you can set up rules as to when and how much money is given to a child and who will be in charge of that money.

Typical plans I prepare include these sorts of provisions:

1. All of the child's inheritance would be held in a trust fund under the control of a trustee chosen by the parent until the child reaches a certain age (for example, twenty-five). Until then, the trustee has the authority and the decision-making discretion to pay for such things as college tuition, books, transportation, medical expenses, or whatever the trustee believes to be a reasonable expense. The child does not decide what to spend the money on. The child can make requests, but the final decisions as to the appropriateness of the requests are those of the trustee.

2. Similar plans would give the child one-third the balance of the trust fund money at age twenty-five, one-third at age thirty, and one-third at age thirty-five—or a similar pattern. There may be authority to make additional distributions to the trust beneficiary if the trustee believes these are appropriate.

3. Some parents put conditions on the distribution of money, such as requiring drug screening of the beneficiaries before they are eligible for a payout. Other conditions can be put in the trust and do not have to be approved by anyone. Some I have seen (but do not necessarily agree with) set up requirements such as attending a particular college, staying a member of a particular church, maintaining a certain grade point average, acting as a missionary

for a certain period of time, getting married by a certain age, and even not getting married before a certain age. There are so many more, limited only by a person's imagination.

The point is that a trust is flexible and can be set up with whatever rules and regulations you want. There are no guidelines so long as the terms are legal. And the money is yours to leave in whatever fashion you choose.

DISABLED BENEFICIARIES

There are millions of disabled people. Disabilities may exist from birth or may be inflicted later on as a result of accident or illness. Mental and physical problems of an heir require that someone else take care of the special needs of the person so that assets are used in the heir's best interests. The disabled person may be perfectly capable of making financial decisions, but leaving that right to them may mean they are disqualified from certain benefits to which they would otherwise be entitled.

Physical or mental disabilities create two needs for a trust.

First, disabled people may not have the mental or physical capacity to handle the ongoing management of their money. Bills need to be paid, money invested, taxes prepared. They may be subject to coercion or undue influence by those who would take the money they rely on, or they may just make bad money management decisions. Having their inheritance left to them in trust, under the control of an independent trustee, solves this problem.

Second, leaving money to a disabled beneficiary is often like leaving them nothing at all.

The reason is that many disabled people rely on state or federal benefit programs for their medical care. Medical care is, of course, very expensive, and most of us would go broke fast having to pay for it without insurance. Nursing home care, for example, can cost in excess of $100,000 per year. A day in the hospital may cost thousands. Certain drugs are unaffordable without help.

Programs like Medicaid are what we call "need-based." This means that the person needing help must qualify based on his or her income and assets. Currently, the law is that if a person has more than $2,000 in assets plus a few other minor things he does not qualify for Medicaid. So if you leave money to a person who is receiving Medicaid, he may no longer qualify because of the amount of inherited money and must spend down the inheritance to the threshold level by paying for his own medical care. Then, when the money is gone, he has to go through the sometimes lengthy process of reapplying for the medical benefits.

I am not making a judgment of right or wrong here, but I can tell you that most people would prefer to leave money to their disabled beneficiaries in such as way as to not disqualify them but still let them benefit from the inherited assets. A properly arranged "special-needs" provision in your trust can do just that. This provision allows the money to be used for things that benefit them during their lifetime, then have the remainder go to some other beneficiary after death. The special-needs provisions have to be carefully written, since the wrong wording can completely throw out the intent of the provisions and make the inheritance subject to spend-down. Also, the beneficiary cannot be his or her own trustee.

SPENDTHRIFTS

We all know people who just cannot hold onto money. If they have it, they spend it. If they can borrow it, they will spend it. Their credit cards are maxed out. They may have declared bankruptcy, had repossessions, or even been sued for non-payment of bills. These people are spendthrifts and will spend their inheritance very quickly if it is not protected for them. There are several ways to handle this.

1. **Allowance.** Leave them a share of the trust assets but have it given to them in a certain amount per month so they do not get a lump sum to waste. Another provision could say where the remainder of the trust funds will go if they die before it is all given to them. A variation on this is to pay out only the interest on the trust funds, with the principal going to someone else—perhaps the grandchildren—at the death of the beneficiary.

2. **Set number of years.** A common method is to have an inheritance paid out in annual installments over five, ten, fifteen, or twenty years. The rationale here is that if the beneficiary makes a mistake with one installment, he will have time to think about it before the next installment comes along. It also solves the problem of someone entering a bad marriage and losing the inherited money along the way.

3. **Retirement accounts.** I see clients who have adult children who are not necessarily bad with money but have poor paying jobs with no retirement plans, have no savings, and therefore have no money for the future. The parents will set up a plan that pays out a percentage at their death and the balance held in trust and invested for them until the beneficiary reaches retirement age—say, sixty-five or sixty-six.

There are many other variations on distributions to spendthrifts that basically manage money for someone who cannot effectively manage it for himself. If you can put together a plan, your attorney can put it in the right legal language.

Similar considerations and plans need to be made for heirs who have substance abuse problems or who are incarcerated. Some states now will go after the assets of an inmate to pay for care.

GAY COUPLES/UNMARRIED COUPLES

An unmarried couple, whether gay or not, needs the protection only a trust can offer. Unmarried couples do not have the legal rights afforded to those who are married. An example: Allen came to see me after his partner William died. They had been together for eighteen years. William had three adult children who seemed to get along with Allen—in fact, they exchanged presents for birthdays and Christmas. Now that William was dead, the relationship had changed and the children were no longer so fond of Allen. It seems the house they lived in was originally William's. They had both paid their share of the mortgage and shared all the other expenses of the house, but Allen's name had never been put on the title. Now, the kids wanted the house. Neither Allen nor William had made out a will or a trust. Allen had no legal rights to live in his own home any longer. This meant that the kids could (and did) rightfully and legally evict Allen. I have also seen the same thing happen several times in heterosexual relationships. While mom or dad is alive, everything is fine, but once death removes them the family relationship quickly turns into a matter of money. The moral is to get some written protection for your partner in your trust documents.

With a trust you can provide your partner with the right to live in the house for his or her lifetime—what we call a life estate or life lease. At your partner's death the kids can sell the house. Or you can provide that the partner has a right to live there for a set period of time, such as one or two years. Often there is a requirement that the bills have to be paid such as mortgage, taxes, insurance, and maintenance in order to have the right to stay in the house. Sometimes provisions are put in that would not allow the surviving partner to rent the house or share it with others. The choice of restrictions and requirements is yours.

Other issues arise such as determining ownership of furniture and other personal property items, and provisions for these should be specifically set out in the trust language. Either partner could make a list of individual items to be given immediately at death to particular people, with the rest of the household goods and furniture going to the survivor. One of the purposes and goals of a well written trust is to avoid problems for surviving partners and beneficiaries. We do this by having an answer to the "what if" questions and making the trust provisions totally unambiguous.

BLENDED FAMILIES

In the typical family unit today, one or both partners may have been previously married and they may both have had children from those prior marriages. Estate planning is an absolute must in these situations. Otherwise, everything may end up in the hands of the children of the spouse who lives the longest.

The first consideration is to be sure your current spouse is protected by the trust provisions. Often, the marital home was owned before the marriage by one spouse or the other. It is not unusual to find the new spouse's name was never put on the title to the property—a big problem, since the new spouse may have to probate the house in order to continue to live in it and may even find that the stepchildren own all or part of it. Having the house in the name of the marital trust assures that the surviving spouse will be able to continue to live in the house without interference from the family.

The second factor is survival. Without a trust or will, the assets will, in most cases, belong to the surviving spouse. At her death, those assets would by law go to her children. So without a trust, it could become a gamble—a matter of who lives the longest—to determine whose children get the joint assets.

A trust can contain very flexible provisions to meet your intentions. For example:

1. At the death of one spouse an immediate distribution of certain assets or money is made to that person's children, with the rest staying in trust for the benefit of the survivor.

2. At the death of one spouse the income from the marital trust assets could be paid out to the survivor as earned, with the remainder at death paid out to all the children of both spouses.

3. The trust could become unchangeable at the death of one spouse to insure that the children of the first spouse to die are not disinherited by the survivor. This means, in effect, that the trust becomes irrevocable at the first death.

4. Most commonly the surviving spouse gets the use and ownership of all the trust assets but cannot change the trust to effectively disinherit the children of the first spouse to die.

Any rules that you think are fair and both agree on can be put into the trust rules and regulations. The above are just a few examples. The point is that if you do not decide now, then state law will decide for you—and you may not like what the law would do.

SEPARATED COUPLES OR SEPARATE TRUSTS

Sometimes both spouses don't agree on what would go into a joint trust and want separate plans funded with their own separate assets. Especially if a couple is separated, each wants to be certain that the trust is not going to be invaded after the death of the first by the survivor. In most states, if both parties agree, the trust assets in separate trusts are not reachable by the survivor except as specifically spelled out in the trust documents. The trust becomes in effect a postnuptial agreement.

With a will, a surviving spouse has rights over and above what the will of the deceased partner set out. In Michigan, for example, there are rights of election, homestead allowances, and exempt property rights—all of which allow a surviving spouse to "break" the will. So, in effect, you cannot disinherit a spouse with a will. You may write a will that says your spouse is supposed to get a certain amount, but the spouse has the right, through probate court, to take what the state would give instead of what the will provides.

A trust does not have that problem in many states, particularly if both spouses agree to abide by the trust terms in writing. This can be done by including the right language in the trust and then having the trust signed by both parties. Beware, however, of one partner fraudulently misrepresenting the nature and extent of his assets to get the other to agree.

In Michigan and some other states, at least under current law, a surviving spouse cannot elect against a trust and is stuck with whatever she is given under the terms of the trust. There are no other options. A trust is a much safer way of assuring that your instructions will be followed.

LARGE ESTATES

Trusts can eliminate or dramatically reduce estate and inheritance taxes. You might think you do not need to worry about estate tax since the threshold right now is $3.5 million, but keep in mind that the IRS considers all assets taxable. So life insurance, retirement plans, and real estate, as well as traditional investments, are considered taxable. I have seen young parents with very little in the way of liquid assets who have multi-million dollar life insurance policies (which are taxable for estate tax purposes at their deaths) and who ended up paying a huge estate tax bill that could have been avoided with a trust.

This is important because it is a big tax. The tax rate is 37 to 45 percent of everything over the threshold (though the rate is also subject to legislative change). So a $4 million estate could have a tax bill of $200,000.

A typical marital trust can have provisions that double the estate tax exemption amount, effectively preserving two exemptions. This is a very inexpensive way of saving potentially huge amounts of tax, without complicating things while you are alive. Some estate planning attorneys are unaware of the type of joint trust that can preserve two estate tax exemptions. If you have just over $3.5 million and your attorney pushes the two-trust plan while being unable to explain why the joint trust with tax exemption doubling alternatives is unavailable to you, perhaps you are speaking to the wrong attorney.

Large estates can also achieve significant estate and income tax savings using the more sophisticated types of trusts, such as charitable remainder trusts, as well as family limited partnerships, limited liability companies, and other complex estate planning techniques. Consult an estate planning expert to develop a plan for you.

Remember that Congress changes the tax laws frequently, so you should keep track of the exemption amount since it may be significantly different from what it was when this book went to press. Having the joint trust with the tax provisions would, however, give you twice the then-current exemption amount, so it is the safest way to go, even if you think you are likely to fall under the single exemption amount.

SMALL ESTATES

Even some very small estates benefit from having a trust. You should refer to chapter 9, where I discuss small estates in detail, but in some cases a trust is called for even if non-trust alternatives are available. For example, you may have only your house, a small savings account, and a life insurance policy to leave your children at your death. These could be handled without a trust and without probate by devices such as joint ownership and beneficiary designations.

But suppose you have one of the categories of concerns I just covered above, such as a disabled child, an unmarried partner, an unequal distribution plan among children, or spendthrift heirs? You can, by using a trust, see that the money available is used for specific purposes, like paying off a child's education loans or tuition, or held for them until they meet certain conditions you set up. Certainly a disabled beneficiary cannot be left more than $2,000 outside a trust without the risk of losing Medicaid benefits. I have had a number of clients who were estranged from their children and even some who have children in prison. They may not want these children to share in the estate, and a trust can easily accomplish this intent. Trusts can be a way of making maximum use of a limited amount of money.

I have had people tell me that they are concerned about the cost of probate in their small estate because of the amount of cost relative to the size of the estate. Paying three or four thousand dollars for probate may be affordable for a $500,000 estate but may seem like a large share of a $100,000 one—especially if there are a lot of heirs. I have seen cases where the attorney got a bigger share of the estate than did the individual beneficiaries after all the probate costs were figured. This should not happen with a trust.

DISABILITY

A trust voids the need for adult guardianship and conservatorship. A guardian is the person who is in charge of caring for a disabled adult, whether due to mental or physical disability, to the point that the person cannot take care of himself. This is done under the authority of the probate court and requires a fairly complex legal process. A petition is filed either by a social agency or family member stating the need for the guardianship.

The court appoints an independent lawyer, a "guardian ad litem" (GAL) for the allegedly incapacitated individual—the ward. This procedure will vary state by state, but the procedure is similar.

The GAL interviews the ward and others who have knowledge about the ward, reports back to the court in writing, and appears in person at a court hearing. All relatives are notified and can attend the hearing or bring their own attorneys. The judge then decides whether the guardianship is needed and if so, appoints a guardian who from then on has to report to the court in writing and in person on how the ward is doing. A conservator—a person appointed by a court to manage the money of another person—is usually appointed at the same time. Minor children may have conservators. Disabled adults may also have conservators. The purpose of the conservatorship is to be sure that the ward's (the person who is in need of the conservatorship) money is being honestly and effectively managed. This is a valuable service for the ward, but it comes at a high cost to the family.

In order to establish a conservatorship for an adult, an interested party petitions the court. This may be a family member, a state agency such as Adult Protective Services, or even a concerned non-family member. They state in writing why they believe the ward needs a conservator. The court then appoints a GAL, typically an attorney or county agency, who visits the ward, investigates the situation, then reports back to the court with a recommendation on whether a conservatorship is needed. Then there is usually a court hearing. Family members and others can testify under oath as to the facts they know relating to the mental state of the ward, giving examples of what the ward may be doing to cause the need for someone else to take over.

This is often a humiliating experience for the ward and embarrassing to the family. The expense is high since the ward has to pay the GAL even if the conservatorship is deemed unnecessary, and the family may hire one or more other attorneys to promote their view of the conservatorship.

It doesn't stop there. If the conservatorship is granted, the conservator charges annual fees for acting as conservator. Further, the assets of the ward may have to be placed in restricted accounts with little opportunity for the best investment management. The conservator has to account to the court annually for everything financial that is done, and may even need individual permission for extraordinary expenses of the ward.

All this is avoided with a trust. The trust has language that defines when a person is to be considered incapacitated, and when that occurs, the alternate or successor trustee immediately steps in and begins managing the assets of the trust owner. When combined with the medical directives and power of attorney that are part of the trust-based estate plan (see chapter 12), there is no need for a court-supervised guardianship and conservatorship. In fact, I have defeated petitions for guardianship in court merely by showing the judge that the proposed ward already had a durable power of attorney as well as a revocable trust with a trustee in place managing the assets.

If you have any of the concerns outlined above, you absolutely must have a trust or the inherited assets are going to be wasted or misused.

CHAPTER THREE

A Comparison: Trusts and Wills

Okay, so what is the truth? Is a will the best choice because it's cheaper? Is it cheaper?

At an estate planning seminar recently, I discussed trusts versus wills with another attorney. He was of the opinion that there was no cost-saving at all in having a trust instead of a will, even if probate was avoided. Therefore, his advice to all but the rich was to use a will. I was very interested in how he arrived at that conclusion.

His reasoning was as follows: He charged a lot of money for the will up-front (so he was not talking about a $250 simple will). His estate plan package using a will plus the durable power of attorney and medical directives was approaching $1,500. He then charged a lot for probate (with his fees at $300 per hour over a year or two of probate for a modest estate, the total would easily cost $5,000 to $10,000).

So does that support my argument for avoiding probate and using a trust? Well, no. He also charged a lot for a trust—typically $2,500 to $3,500. Then he charged a lot for what he called "trust settlement"—again at $300 per hour—and it took a long time to complete the process since his office did virtually everything to carry out the trust terms. So using this lawyer saved no money or time at all. He was creating a huge fee no matter how the estate was handled. In his case, he was right: There was no advantage to the trust. More on avoiding this kind of lawyer in chapter 5.

A very nice trust that will meet nearly everyone's needs can be had for a very reasonable price—much less than Mr. Lawyer was charging in the previous paragraph. You have to do your homework, interview lawyers, get referrals, go to seminars—all the techniques for finding the right lawyer I outline in chapter 5. If you do that, you will find that the initial cost of setting up the trust is practically the only legal fee you will ever pay. The reason is that trust settlement is not legal work. It is mostly clerical work. You do not need to pay $300 an hour to a lawyer to settle a trust if you know what to do.

Trust settlement is the process of carrying out the instructions in the trust as to who gets what and when. The typical chores must be done of identifying what debts have to be paid, publishing notice in the newspaper, getting an IRS number to open a bank account, selling assets, filing claims for life insurance, and so forth, but these are not legal work and do not require a lawyer.

What you need are instructions to the trustee upon death of the trust owner. Most lawyers are not going to give these instructions to you. They keep this process a secret. But I am going to tell you how to do it step-by-step in this book's final chapter. In fact, in every trust-based estate plan I have done, there is a section on trustee instructions, which, if followed, allow a quick and easy settlement of the trust with no legal costs at all. Am I shooting myself in the foot? True, I don't charge for trust settlement very often but I have plenty to do creating trusts by referral from satisfied clients.

Using a will and probating it, however, is definitely legal work; plus, it is time-consuming and therefore expensive. Most people cannot do their own probate. True, much of it is computerized, using software packages and fill-in-the-blank forms, but only lawyers have these or know how to use them. The probate system and probate laws are also geared toward making it take a long time. Completing a probate case in less than six months is nearly impossible because of the way the system is set up with its waiting periods and notice and publication requirements, and oftentimes court hearings that may be required.

Probate is an attorney's bread and butter—kind of like the slot machines that pay the rent in Vegas.

In fact, if you live in a state like California or Florida, the laws do not even allow you to do probate without a lawyer. They say that every personal representative (think executor) must be represented by a lawyer. So you couldn't do it yourself, even if you wanted to. Most everybody subject to probate in those states should have a trust.

It used to be, and still is in some states, true that probate had one advantage that trusts did not: a short statute of limitations. This means that by publishing a notice in the local newspaper to potential creditors of the deceased, you can limit how long any creditor has to present a claim against the probate estate to four, six, or nine months.

Years ago, other attorneys and I would intentionally put parts of certain estates through probate just to get this short statute of limitations. An example:

Say I owned an estate with a deceased surgeon. We would not want the estate held open and subject to possible lawsuits for malpractice until the normal negligence statute of limitations expired in maybe a year or two, so by having part of his estate probated we could shut the door on any possible claims that might be out there and get the estate finalized. The rest of the estate would be handled by the trust.

I don't worry about that anymore. In 2010, Michigan joined 22 other states in adopting a form of the Uniform Trust Act, which gives trusts the same sort of protection wills have always enjoyed. So now we never probate estates for statute of limitation reasons. Included in my set of instructions to the trustee in the last chapter is a fill-in-the-blank publication notice that the trustee runs one time in the newspaper to get the four-month statute of limitations for the trust, thereby canceling the only advantage of probate over trusts. You might want to use this even if your state does not officially recognize the validity of the trust notice publication as a way of identifying unknown creditors.

The availability of publication to shorten the statute of limitations may not exist in your state. If you are like most people, the danger of having a claim presented after the trust is settled is slim to none. Most of us know what the debts are. However, if you are in a high-risk occupation or have been involved in numerous business dealings that might or could lead to litigation, having one small part of your estate probated will give you that protection. The rest of your assets can pass through the trust.

Sometimes there are problems in trusts that require a judge to sort them out, but not often. It is very rare for a trust to end up in court; however, if a trustee needs the assistance of the court for some reason, the probate court has the authority to administer and oversee trusts on request of an interested party.

REAL ESTATE IN MORE THAN ONE STATE

It is not unusual to see people who own real estate in multiple states, such as a winter home in Florida and a summer home in the north. With a will, probate would be necessary in both states. New York courts do not have the legal authority to probate real estate in Florida or any other state. So we have for a New York resident what is called "ancillary probate" in Florida, which is basically a companion probate. It effectively then doubles the cost of probate. I had a client with real estate in five different states—big trouble without a trust. And ancillary probate can be expensive. The attorney handling it has no relationship with the family, will not likely see any of their business again, and therefore may charge the maximum going rate for the probate.

With a trust, all the real estate from every state can be put into one trust ownership using a quit-claim deed and there is no probate in any state. The trustee merely hires an attorney in the companion state to do a deed from the trust to the beneficiaries, or the trustee sells the property in the other state through the trust. No probate and no expenses other than realtor and closing fees.

Huge savings in time, trouble, and money.

FAMILY HARMONY

Wills can cause family trouble. There are two reasons for this. First, probate takes a long time to complete, from seven months to several years depending upon what problems arise. Because of this time delay, heirs become suspicious of the executor and the attorney for the estate. I have heirs come to see me who think they should have their own lawyer in the probate just to protect their interests. They ask me, "How do I know for sure that the executor is doing the right things without somebody on my side?"

When you get two or more lawyers involved, the costs begin to go up. You are paying a lawyer for results. They want to appear to be doing something for you, so they bill hours, write letters, do research, and make telephone calls. Law is a game of adversaries with each lawyer fighting for his or her client. It causes trouble, expense, and hard feelings. Your lawyer is not doing his job unless he can point to something he accomplished. It may be that all he has to do is monitor the proceedings, but that is not the way it usually works out.

Second, wills are fairly easy to contest. When a probate case is opened, a court file number is given to it, a judge is assigned to the case, and easy-to-use court forms are made available for filing motions and setting up hearings. Attorney fees are what the court calls priority claims. In other words, the lawyers get paid first, so there is a pot of money out of which attorneys can collect their fees. Attorneys do not expect a big up-front retainer in a will contest. Contesting a trust is a different matter, however. Attorneys will expect a retainer fee and will bill against that at their normal hourly rates, win or lose. Having to come up with cash is a disincentive to contesting a trust.

This ease of contesting a will leads to will contest extortion. Executors often settle a specious claim against a will just because it is often cheaper and quicker than trying to fight over it. There are some—not many, but some—lawyers who engage in this blackmail game and are rarely called on it. There are court rules that are supposed to prevent this from happening, but they are rarely enforced.

Remember that the cost of probate is not what lawyers would lead you to believe. It is not the state, the court system, taxes, or "court costs" that run up the cost of probate. It is almost entirely attorney fees.

Trust settlement without an attorney can be done quickly and with no legal costs. Because everything is wrapped up so fast, there is not much time for heirs to worry about the process. You basically gather together the assets, pay the bills, file the last year's income tax return, and distribute the assets to the heirs—that's it. No papers to file with a court or the state, no fees to pay.

No-contest clauses and arbitration clauses also limit challenges to trusts. A no-contest clause is a paragraph or two that says that anyone who challenges the trust, even if they are successful, would get only one dollar as their inheritance. While this clause is not a bar to challenging a trust on the basis that the maker of the trust was senile or otherwise incompetent when they made the trust, the fact that the provision is there stops a lot of trust contests. It's kind of like the sign in the parking garage that says they are not responsible for loss or damage to your car. The sign itself discourages people from suing even if the garage might have been legally responsible.

Similarly an arbitration provision can slow down contests. This provision says that if someone wants to challenge the trust or any part of it they must first submit to arbitration to settle their claim and if unsuccessful must pay for the arbitration fees of both sides. That one is a real stopper. Arbitration is like a mini trial of all the issues. It can cost a lot, take a lot of time, and the outcome is uncertain. Plus there is the no-contest provision that may be enforceable, so even if the other side wins, they may get nothing. Personally, I like this arbitration provision.

To contest a trust, the one contesting must hire and pay for a lawyer out of his own pocket. There is no probate court priority for attorney fees and it can be difficult to find a lawyer willing to take on a trust contest on a contingency fee basis (getting their attorney fees out of the winnings). Trusts are a more certain way of seeing that your intentions and instructions are carried out at death and are not thwarted by litigation.

PRIVACY

Probate files are public record. Many people are not aware of this, but anyone can go to the courthouse, look at any court file, and find out who inherited what and how much they got. I heard of a car dealer years ago who gleaned the names of heirs from probate files so he could try to sell them cars. "I hear you came into some money. I have a heck of a deal on a new Cadillac for you." Seems sleazy, but it is perfectly legal.

A trust is private. No one other than the heirs know what anyone inherited, what restrictions there might be, or even the size of the estate. Most of us want this information private, and a trust keeps it that way. (Although if, in that one-in-a-hundred case, the trust gets filed with the court, then it can be made public record too.)

The privacy aspect also makes it harder to contest since only the heirs involved can get a look at the paperwork.

CHAPTER FOUR

Trust Seminars:
A Free Dinner, But at What Cost?

Every week I receive at least one invitation by mail or telephone to attend a free dinner at a local hotel or restaurant. These folks seem to have the AARP mailing list. The invitation is typically from a stock broker, financial planner, attorney, or estate planner. The point of the dinner is ostensibly to give me information important to me on estate taxes, guardianships, how to avoid probate, taking care of my IRAs, and so on.

I actually go to some of these dinner seminars just to see what people are being told and what they are being sold. Most of them are in the same vein—a slide presentation narrated by up to three speakers for the purpose of convincing the audience that they need to get their financial affairs and estate planning in order, or else! Some of them have exaggerated claims of the time and expense of probate to scare people into signing up with them. Some have information that is downright incorrect. I attended one seminar run by an attorney who was so far off-base in his advice that I was tempted to stand up in the back of the room and tell the audience not to listen to this guy because he did not know what he was talking about.

Everyone at the seminars knows that the agenda of the presenters is to sell something. Whether it is long-term care insurance, brokerage services, legal documents, or annuities, they are not feeding you for nothing.

I am reminded of my mother, who has a closet full of umbrellas and tries to give me one every time I visit.

"Where did you get all these umbrellas?" I asked the first time.

She replied, "The Buick dealer down the street gives me an umbrella and a hot dog every Sunday if I take a test drive."

Mom was never going to buy a Buick and I think the dealer knew that, but sales is a numbers game—get in front of enough people and some will buy. It's the same thing with these seminars. Some people go to all the ones they are invited to just to get the free meal. But some of the guests are new and some of them eventually get convinced.

I have been approached by a number of companies over the years who put on these seminars. They ask me if they can refer their customers to me to prepare a trust-based estate plan for them. I have to very carefully investigate companies making such requests. Some are good, and some are downright crooked. As a consumer you have to be cautious with whom you deal in financial and legal matters, particularly when you are revealing your personal financial and family information to them.

So here is the criterion you should look at in deciding whether to attend a trust seminar: **Who is putting on the seminar?**

Attorneys may hold workshops or seminars as a way of attracting new clients. The information is usually good and what is being sold are the attorney's services for preparing a trust, powers of attorney, and funding services. The attorney cannot sell annuities or insurance, so you are not going to be pressured on those fronts. He may try to get you to sign up for an office conference or may even visit you in your home to wrap up the details.

What to watch out for: Just because they are putting on a seminar does not mean they know what they are doing or are charging you a fair price. See the next chapter on attorneys for more about that. Check out the attorney: How long has he been in practice? How many trusts does he do every year? How long will it take to get the trust done? Be sure you have a written fee agreement and that you know in advance what the total costs will be. Do not agree to an hourly rate. An agreed-upon flat rate for the entire service should be in writing.

Are you a member of a prepaid legal services plan? Some attorneys participate in these plans and can do all of your estate planning at no cost to you. In my office, for example, you get exactly the same documents and services if you have legal insurance as you would if you were paying cash. I have seen some attorneys, though, that give their clients the stripped-down version if it's through a legal plan.

Brokers, financial planners, and insurance agents will discuss living trusts, guardianships, and so forth—and may even have an attorney to whom they refer you—but their primary goal is to sell you annuities, long-term care insurance, or other investments. They may want to sign you up as a client and charge a fee for financial planning advice. Often they want to rework your IRA. Remember that they make a commission on anything they do, and be sure that you are getting advice based on your best interest rather than the agent's. Be certain that any change they make in your investments, including your IRAs and retirement accounts, is not going to reduce the value of that account or put unacceptable restrictions on your access to your own funds. A good way of protecting yourself is to listen to what they have to say, then run their recommendations past another person in the same business. The money you have now is not easily replaced if lost in a bad investment, especially when you are retired.

Trust sales companies are a mixed bag. Seminars are being run throughout the country by big organizations to sell you on a living trust and all the related documents. The presentations are slick and the sales techniques high-pressure. There are sometimes no local attorneys involved in the preparation of the legal documents at all—often the legal work is done in another state by the company employees and then shipped back to the salesman for delivery to you. The trusts are generic, not necessarily appropriate for you, hard to understand, and overpriced. I know all this because I have seen dozens of these trusts brought to me for a review of validity.

Beware of any company that claims it is selling you legal documents if the people are not themselves attorneys. It is illegal in most states for a non-attorney to give legal advice, to prepare someone's estate plan for him, or to sell legal documents specifically designed for you. They may say attorneys are preparing the documents, but if the attorney fees are included in what you pay them, this is illegal, unethical, and may involve no attorney at all.

Illegally selling you legal documents at an inflated price is not the end of it. They use the trust as a way of getting you to reveal all your personal financial information and then try to sell you investments on which they receive big commissions. Some of these companies have been prosecuted for tactics like these, but they often just open up under another name and keep going. The free dinner is not worth the risk of being talked into a bad deal. These salespeople are very convincing.

Trust service companies are different from the trust sales companies and are up-front and completely reputable. A trust service company is not selling you a trust. It may offer you a list of local attorneys from which you can choose to discuss preparing a trust for you, but it does not prepare any legal documents itself or give legal advice. You can use your existing trust with them or even use your own attorney.

What you buy from these companies is typically a service package wherein they agree to help you "fund" your trust (see chapter 8), meet with you annually to be sure your trust is still properly funded, help you fill out a request to amend your trust (which you can send to your attorney to make changes you may want), and even assist the family after your death in submitting claims for life insurance and rolling over retirement plans.

Is their service worth what they charge? It depends, of course, on how good you are at keeping track of your assets yourself. In my experience, as I discuss later, trusts are less likely to be fully funded the older they are, so part of the estate sometimes ends up being probated even when there is a trust. However, with the trust service companies, which provide an annual review, it is rare to have any assets left out at death that need to be probated.

I have dealt with one company out of Texas since 2001 and I am happy to say I have had practically no probate problems with their referred clients primarily due to the annual review process. They do what they say they are going to do. It is not inexpensive, but in the long run, I believe it is a very valuable service to have the trust reviewed annually. Any changes that need to be made would be done by an attorney, but the service company can help with getting newly acquired assets transferred to the trust.

Keep in mind that you are not buying legal documents from a trust service company. They are not lawyers and cannot give legal advice, act as agents for a lawyer, or sell you legal documents. You are buying their services. Also, they sell things such as long-term care insurance and annuities, but you are under no obligation to buy anything at all from them or to let them manage any of your investments or assets. That is always your choice. Be careful of companies that lead you to believe the fees you are paying them are for a trust. The attorney is the only one who can do the trust and will charge you separately for those services.

Check out the company you are thinking of dealing with. Call the Better Business Bureau. Ask for references from other customers they may have serviced. Be sure that you have a signed contract specifying exactly what you are paying for and that you have the right to a "cooling off" period, during which you have the right to cancel while you think it over.

I recommend that you also involve your adult children, if any, in order that they can understand what you have done and what their role will be at your death. Have one or more of the children present when you go over your legal documents. A reputable company or attorney will not discourage the children's participation.

On seminars, my view has always been that I am looking for education and information. Whether I buy anything or make an appointment for more information is secondary and requires a lot of thought and investigation. The same should be true of hiring an attorney.

CHAPTER FIVE

Watch Out for Attorneys

I will make two points in this chapter: the role of attorneys in preparing your estate planning and their role in wrapping up your estate at your death. Both require careful consideration on your part to avoid complications, time delays, and excessive cost to you and your heirs.

Attorneys play a vital role in planning your estate and it would be a mistake to try to avoid them. True, you may be able to put together a trust from something you download off the Internet or from forms you buy at the office supply store, but you would have no assurance that what you have done is going to be legally sufficient and accomplish the goals you have in mind. In particular, the online forms may be specific to the state in which they are sold, and you have no idea who created them or if they will work for you. I am always amazed that people will risk everything they have acquired by putting it into a form from a book—without having expert legal advice—in order to save a bit of money. The old penny-wise-pound-foolish mistake.

The need for independent legal advice is why I have not included fill-in-the-blank forms in this book. There is no one trust that is right for everyone. We all have differing intentions, goals, finances, family relationships, and problems. In my office I use computers, but have developed about sixty separate trust formats for differing situations. Even so, I always have to adapt each one for each client's particular situation.

How to choose the attorney and what to watch out for is very important. I see too many people who do not ask questions, assuming that because the attorney has a law license she will not only know about trusts and estate planning but will treat them fairly. True sometimes, but not always. I see a lot of very poorly made trusts done by attorneys that I am sure the clients paid for in good faith.

There are also advantages to having the guidance of an attorney through all phases of your lifelong estate planning and assisting your family in wrapping up your estate. With regular contact, the attorney (if he is doing the right things for you) can be sure that your trust reflects your current wishes, takes care of you in case of disability, and provides for an orderly and efficient distribution of your assets at your death. These services come with a cost, but a good lawyer will make the investment worthwhile. Of course, you have to have a good lawyer to begin with and would be wise to know what to watch out for in hiring one, so here are my tips and warnings from having seen from the inside what attorneys do since 1975.

WHAT ARE LEGAL SERVICES?

Lawyers charge a lot of money for what they do, but for the legal things that only a lawyer can do, these fees are not necessarily unreasonable. Only a licensed attorney can give specific legal advice, represent a person in court, or prepare legal documents. For these services, attorneys receive years of training and education, which justify the fees charged. They also assume responsibility for the rightness of their legal services and can be sued for attorney malpractice if they are wrong.

Non-attorneys cannot legally do any of those three things. The problem in the estate planning area is that many of the services attorneys charge for are not legal services—they are clerical services. You pay for the attorney's time whether she is in court or just talking to you on the telephone, so your legal fees for the trust could be inflated because of these additional charges. For example, assistance in funding your trust is not all legal in nature. Changing the beneficiary on life insurance so that the trust is the beneficiary rather than a person can be done by anyone. Should you pay hundreds of dollars an hour to have an attorney request a beneficiary change form from the insurance company and fill it out for you? This is clerical work, not legal work. I suggest that when you interview your attorney you ask to do some of the non-legal work yourself if you want to save some money. Same with changing beneficiaries on retirement accounts and annuities—you can do this yourself with no legal assistance.

I know attorneys who will do all the trust funding for a client and charge the normal attorney fee rate for doing it. They have the client sign a power of attorney allowing them to access their financial affairs, then contact the client's banks, credit unions, brokers, and insurance companies to see that all the assets get into the trust. This is a great service but not something you cannot do yourself with the right instructions. I provide my clients with trust funding instructions so they can do the funding without paying me. (See chapter 12.)

Trusts are so common nowadays that the financial institutions know what you need to do and will in most cases do the funding paperwork for you. Trust service companies can assist in the funding as can your financial planner or accountant. You do not have to pay the lawyer to do these things. If saving money on attorney fees is not important to you, then go ahead and let the lawyer do it—but know that you are paying attorney fee rates for clerical services.

WHEN YOUR WILL IS WORTHLESS

Clients often call the lawyer's office because they have been told that they should have a will. Everybody should have a will, people say, and if you do not have one it is because you are procrastinating or are negligent or uncaring toward your family. That is the common feeling, but of course it is not necessarily true; in fact, few people actually need a will. Many need a trust, as we know from the information in this book, but wills are often superfluous if there is no trust.

The most common example I see is the situation where a lawyer prepares a will for a client, which is of no value at all. State laws have what they call laws of "intestacy." This means a set of laws that determine who inherits a person's property if he dies without a will or trust.

Typically, if a person dies leaving no spouse, his children share equally in whatever the deceased owned at death after all expenses are paid. If a will is made out saying that all the assets are to be divided equally among the children, then the will has accomplished nothing. Whether with a will or without, the estate would have to go through probate. Having a will does not make probate simpler, cheaper, or shorter. So in this case, the attorney who makes a will that mirrors the intestacy laws is charging the client for nothing.

Some things may be put in the will that would not be covered by intestacy, which would make the will valuable, such as an unequal distribution among children or disinheriting a child. As explained earlier, a trust can contain all the provisions to set up a testamentary trust. But wills have to be probated and trusts do not, so there is no advantage to the will.

Just before this book went to press, I had a client come in asking for advice about her mother's trust. After that was finished, I asked her what plans she had made for her own estate. She said she was all set—she had a will. After I explained the difference between wills and trusts, she said she had originally asked the lawyer for a trust but he told her that all estates had to be probated, so a will was all she could get. I was astounded at the incorrect advice and prepared a trust for her. I suspect that the attorney knew nothing about trusts but did know about wills and probate and did not want to lose a client. I also think his advice constituted legal malpractice.

HOW MUCH SHOULD A TRUST COST?

Putting a suggested cost for a trust into this book would not be a good thing to do. The cost of legal services varies by where you live, what services are actually being provided, and the attorney who is doing the work. Any price I might put in this book will not necessarily be accurate either where you live or when you read this, though some other books on trusts do give estimates ranging around $3,500, which may be right for your area—but may also be higher or lower than the average where you live.

The important point to you is knowing in advance what you are paying and what services are being performed. You should be able to get a flat fee for a set amount of services. If you require more services than are agreed upon, expect to be charged more. If there are parts of the process you can do yourself, such as getting beneficiary change forms or doing other parts of the trust funding, then you should expect to save some money.

It is unlikely that a lawyer will tell you over the telephone what he charges for a trust, since there are so many different things that may enter into a price determination. That being said, certain trust service companies and financial planners have informal agreements with attorneys to reduce prices for referred clients with the understanding that the financial planner will provide some of the non-legal services such as information gathering, notarization of documents, and trust funding. It is worth looking into.

Also, watch out for a practice I've seen used once in a while: a fee based upon how much the lawyer saves you in estate taxes. There are attorneys who use the standard marital "A/B" trust (see chapter 10), which automatically doubles the estate tax exemption at the death of one spouse. They then run a calculation showing the estate taxes that would occur without that kind of trust, and then base their fee on a percentage of the savings.

Sort of sounds okay if you figure estate taxes would be $250,000 without the trust and nothing with the trust. So paying the lawyer $25,000 to save $250,000 is a good deal, right? Wrong. The A/B trust being used to get this saving is the same one used by most attorneys charging a flat rate of $2,500. There is no special expertise being offered by the lawyer working on a percentage, and in my view, the big fee is excessive and unethical. But it still happens and most clients are not the wiser.

SELECTING A LAWYER TO DO YOUR TRUST

A referral from a satisfied client or a trusted financial planner is the best way. If you do not have either of those, then you need to interview your attorney based on these factors:

Find an expert. While legally, any attorney can prepare your trust, very few have any expertise in this area. In some states, the Bar Association can certify attorneys as experts or specialists in certain areas. Other states, like Michigan, do not accredit specialties at all.

It is possible for a non-specialist to create a good trust. It is also a gamble on your part. The lawyer who tries to handle everything, including divorces, bankruptcies, criminal cases, real estate, personal injury, and estate planning is not likely to be as familiar with trusts as is the attorney who only does trusts and probate. The specialist can determine what you need, give you the right advice, and prepare your documents faster and usually cheaper than can the non-specialist, who may have to research unfamiliar (to her) areas of law for you. Do not pay for the lawyer's education; find someone who already knows what to do.

Part of my legal practice is reviewing the trust previously prepared by another attorney for a client and writing an opinion letter based on it. I tell the client what is right and wrong with their trust, and if there are problems, what needs to be done to correct them. I have reviewed hundreds of trusts over the years drafted by other attorneys, and frankly, I am appalled by the poor quality of legal work that goes on.

My experience is that many attorneys are using fill-in-the-blank trusts that they receive from bank trust departments, buy from legal document companies, or are given at seminars they attend. These are computer programs where the attorney fills in the names of the client, their children, the trustees, and other things specific to the client, and then prints it up. Sometimes the programmed trust chosen by the attorney is not at all appropriate for the client's needs.

I remember several years ago a client brought her trust into my office and dropped it on my desk with a loud thump. It was in a large three-ring binder, about 350 pages long, all boilerplate. When I looked at it, I pointed out to her that the only places in the whole document where her name or the names of her children and trustee appeared were on page 1 and page 350. The rest was basically just filler. She wanted a new one she could understand. The new trust I prepared for her was twenty-seven pages long, and she understood it.

Some of the trust formats I see again and again. A local bank used to hand out computer disks and manuals with the trust they wanted attorneys to use. A lot of attorneys took them and still use them today. One of the priciest attorneys in town uses this trust and charges what I consider outrageous attorney fees for something she did not even write.

I am not suggesting that trusts prepared in this way are never any good. They may work perfectly well, and in fact, some of them were developed by experts in the field who are sharing these with other attorneys in the hope of improving the quality of legal work out there. I am just letting you know that your trust was not written just for you, and you should keep that in mind when you write the check.

There is no specific format for a trust. I can write a perfectly legal trust on one page, though I do not do that for a number of reasons. Trusts do not have to be notarized or even witnessed in some states (though we usually do both of these), so trusts can be made overly simple or overly complicated. I like to make them complete enough to cover what is reasonably likely to happen but not so complex as to make them incomprehensible and unusable.

Ask outright how many trusts the attorney has done in the past and how many he typically creates in a month. Ask him how many wills he makes. The wills should be a small fraction of the trusts if you are talking to the right attorney.

ADVERTISING AND WEB SITES

A lawyer's advertisement is written by the lawyer or his staff. It is an advertisement, not an endorsement by anyone. The lawyer with the biggest ad is not necessarily your best choice. I was one of the first attorneys to advertise in the United States back in 1977. It made the newspapers, since lawyers were previously prohibited from advertising. I had two years experience and did a little of everything. Business boomed. I did not profess to be an expert but just listed the kinds of cases I could do. Other lawyers were furious, saying I was demeaning the legal profession. Actually, I think they did not like to see the apple cart upset. That all changed. The lawyers that criticized me for advertising began advertising themselves and now have the big, full-page, color ads for their firms.

Thirty years later, I no longer advertise. I have one line with my name and telephone number in the telephone directory, and that is all. My directory has about twenty pages of full-page ads for other lawyers and hundreds of smaller display ads. None of these is in any way an indication of the quality of the attorney running the ad. What you can learn from the ads, though, is information such as how long the lawyer has been in practice and whether he concentrates his law just estate planning or tries to do everything. Armed with that information, you can then proceed to interview to decide if they are right for you—kind of like dating.

Web sites are another form of advertising. The Internet is a dangerous place to get information. I recently ran across an attorney Web site filled with information on trusts. The attorney advised that trusts could not reduce taxes (wrong), that lawyers still had to be paid at death (wrong again), that many people were better off with a will due to statute of limitations issues (wrong in many states), and that probate still had to be done in many cases to cover personal property (wrong in most states).

Lawyers' Web sites are written by lawyers for the most part, and the information in them may be true in the particular jurisdiction where the lawyer is located but probably does not apply to everyone everywhere. The lawyer, in fact, may be wrong in her facts altogether. Nobody checks the accuracy of these sites.

Sometimes I think some of them are written to steer people away from trusts and toward wills and probate, where the real money is. Again, though, viewing biographical information about the lawyer herself can be helpful in making a choice.

The lesson for you is not to take what is listed on a Web site as necessarily accurate information, even if it is a lawyer Web site.

TRICKS

Well, maybe not tricks, but practices attorneys engage in that may not be in your best interests.

"My lawyer said I do not need a trust. A will is just fine for me."

I hear this fairly often from clients who have been referred to me by financial planners and others. There are two reasons, I think, why an attorney would tell a client they do not need a trust.

The first is ignorance. Many attorneys have had not training in trusts at all, since they attended law school and took one course on trusts and estates. Trusts are a small part of that and the course may have focused primarily on the history of trusts and the tax reasons for having a trust. Thus, the attorney truly and honestly believe that trusts are for wealthy people who need to minimize or avoid estate and inheritance tax. They have not read chapter 2 of this book and do not realize the importance of trusts for most people.

The second reason is related to the first in a sense. Attorneys know how to make wills and how to probate an estate. Most do not know about trusts and have never settled an estate using a trust or acted as a trustee—I actually prepare trusts for other attorneys who are not familiar with them.

There may be an element of self-interest in trying to develop and maintain a probate practice with some attorneys. As I stated in my introduction, attorneys are taught to build their probate practice with a will file and will safe. It may be cynical to suggest that a lot of attorneys specifically steer people toward probate rather than trusts just for the money involved, but I can assure you that some do.

How do you keep clients and build up your probate practice (which is very lucrative)? One traditional method is to have a will safe (a locking file cabinet where clients' original wills are kept). After the will signing ceremony the lawyer gives the client a nice photocopy and holds the original for safekeeping. At the death of the client, the executor has to go back to the lawyer to get the will for probate and nine times out of ten will hire the lawyer to do the probate. Good business. Some attorneys even have themselves written into the will as attorneys for the estate or as executors. Why do you think the will envelope has the law firm name, address, and telephone number on it? So the family will know who to call to do the probate. Again, good business.

MY WILL DOES NOT HAVE TO GO THROUGH PROBATE

I hear this a lot, particularly from older clients (my age). For some reason, a lot of people believe that a will does not have to be probated. Well, in some cases that may be true—for example, if one spouse dies and the couple's property is all jointly owned, there may be nothing separately owned by the deceased to probate. But at the death of the survivor, probate would be absolutely necessary for all the assets left in the survivor's name.

I had a client point out to me the specific language in the will that clearly said it did not have to be probated. Here is the paragraph:

"It is my strongest intent that my estate not be subject to supervised probate court administration, and I therefore direct that such intent be followed as permitted by the Michigan Estates and Protected Individuals Code, or as may be available under current law."

Sounds like no probate. But that is not what it really says. It says that the client does not want "Supervised Probate Court Administration." In Michigan, there are two basic ways to probate and estate: an informal procedure and a formal procedure. Saying you do not want the supervised administration just means that you want the unsupervised form. It is still probate and it still takes a long time and costs a lot of money. Unsupervised, though, is easier for the lawyer. I think clients interpret this paragraph to mean what it seems to say rather than what it really means.

THE ATTORNEY ANNUAL REVIEW

I said before in the trust services section that an annual review is a good idea to keep the trust funded and up to date with a client's wishes. That was said in the context of a service, which provided that review for your lifetime for a one-time flat fee.

Paying an attorney for an annual review is not always necessary. I know there are attorneys who act like dentists, setting annual appointments for all their clients to go over their estate planning. In most cases, nothing needs to be done. That will be $300—see you next year!

You should contact your attorney in the following situations:

1. Someone involved in the trust has died or has become disabled and is receiving governmental benefits.

2. You have changed your mind about who will get what after you die.

3. You have changed your mind about who will be in charge of your trust at your death or upon your disability.

4. You have new real estate to transfer into your trust and need to have a deed prepared (see chapter 8 on funding the trust).

5. Your financial situation has dramatically changed or you are starting a new business.

Most of the time this is not going to be an annual event. You may have several years go by during which you need no changes to your legal documents. The forced annual review is typically not needed. A good lawyer will let you know if there are changes in the law that necessitate a change in your documents and planning.

THE WILL AS A WAY TO FUND THE TRUST

One of the really reprehensible things I have seen done (this is my opinion, attorneys, so don't sue me) in trust practice by lawyers is using the pour-over will as a way to fund the trust.

A "pour-over will" is a will that says if there are assets left in your name at your death that are not either in your trust or that pass to your trust under some sort of beneficiary or pay-on-death designation, you want those assets to be given to your trust after probate is complete—in other words, to "pour over" into your trust to be handled like any other trust asset. So it is meant as a back-up document, just in case you forget to fund your trust with something.

But some lawyers view the pour-over will as the funding mechanism for the trust. They put nothing at all into the trust during your lifetime. It is unfunded. Then, at your death, they probate the pour-over will and transfer the assets to the trust, before taking care of settling the trust.

This is a great deal for the lawyer. She can charge for creating the trust, creating the will, probating the estate, and settling the trust. There are a lot of attorney fees there—it's like getting paid twice for the same thing.

When properly done, there is a completely funded trust with no assets in the name of the deceased at death and no probate is necessary. With the instructions to the trustee I have included in the last chapter, your trustee should not need a lawyer at all at your death and should have no legal expenses beyond the creation of the original trust and any amendments that were made since then.

CHAPTER SIX

Trustees

A trustee is someone you can trust—someone who will take charge of your trust documents after your death and carry out your wishes. What does a trustee typically do? Not only the financial things such as gathering together investments, insurance death benefits, and selling real estate, but the more mundane things like cleaning out the garage and basement, making funeral arrangements, doing your final income tax returns, and paying any leftover bills. So while it does take some time, most of these duties do not require the services of a lawyer. Following the instructions in this book will make the job quite easy for most trustees.

How can you be sure your trustee can be trusted? There are ways to be more certain your trustee does the job faithfully and honestly. One good way is to name two trustees as co-trustees to act together, especially if it is a blended family in which each parent has a separate set of children. Taking one child from each side of the family creates a situation where they watch each other and are more likely to do things properly.

In situations where there are no trustworthy people with whom you are comfortable, you can have a provision put in your trust that the trust is to be registered with the probate court for supervision. (The name of the court handling probate cases is different in some states. It may also be called a circuit court, superior court, district court, but it is the court that handles the estates of deceased people.)

The law calls this trustee a "fiduciary" and as such, imposes on the trustee certain legal obligations. A trustee is bound by the terms of the trust but also by the state law governing fiduciaries.

For example, there is in most states a set of laws commonly known as the "Prudent Investor Rules." These basically say that a trustee must be conservative and careful in managing the assets of the trust. The trustee must not put the trust assets in jeopardy by making risky investments. The trustee has statutory obligations to keep good accounting records and keep the trust beneficiaries informed as to what is happening with the trust. You need an organized trustee who keeps good records, so it is very important to choose the correct trustee.

Years ago, it was common to choose professional trustees— usually the trust department of a local bank. That still happens, but typically for larger trusts. The problem with professional trustees, in my experience, is that they are not too willing to exercise their discretionary power to make distributions to beneficiaries.

As an example, I was contacted by a twenty-one-year-old college student who was the beneficiary of the trust of her deceased grandfather. The bank was the trustee and the trust said that the beneficiary was entitled to use the money for "educational purposes" and any other expense that the bank thought appropriate. There was about $1.5 million in the trust account. The student had requested money to buy a used car since she wanted to live off-campus in an area with no bus service. The bank refused to give her anything for a car, saying that was an inappropriate and non-educational expense. Had her parents been the trustees instead of the bank she probably would have gotten the money since it was not, in my view, unreasonable.

Most people choose family members as trustees to simplify things and keep the costs down.

YOU (AND/OR SPOUSE) AS TRUSTEE

The trustee is the one who is in charge of the trust. In most cases, the grantor (the maker and owner of the trust) is his own trustee during his lifetime. Couples usually have joint trusts or are co-trustees. If one of the couple dies, the survivor usually remains the sole trustee until death or disability.

After both grantors die or are incapable of acting as trustees, the "successor trustee(s)" takes over as trustee. The successor trustee is not a grantor and cannot change the terms of the trust in most cases but can only carry out the terms of the trust put in place by the grantor (though there are special situations where trust provisions can be changed by a court or a "trust protector" described later).

The trust becomes irrevocable (unchangeable) after the death or disability of the grantors but is revocable (changeable) during their lifetimes so long as they are capable and competent. These are the general rules. However, people often have reasons to do things differently.

For example, one of the two grantors may have been the financial manager and the other grantor may not be capable of handling the business decision-making that a trustee needs to be able to do. In that case the trust may provide that at the death of the financially capable grantor, another person will act as either sole trustee for the surviving grantor or as a co-trustee with the survivor.

Sometimes a couple wants to be certain that a survivor will not be tempted to misuse the trust assets in such a way as to thwart the intentions of the first grantor to die. In that case a co-trustee may be named along with the survivor just to be certain that trust transactions are being done properly and honestly according to the terms both grantors set up when alive. This method unfortunately can cause friction between the survivor and the co-trustee, because the survivor is no longer solely in charge of her financial affairs. But it is a pretty much guaranteed way of assuring that the trust rules are followed since all trust transactions require two signatures.

Bank trustees typically charge 1 to 1.5 percent of the trust assets annually as a fee for serving as trustee. Family members who are also beneficiaries usually do it for free however, it is not uncommon to specify a payment to a trustee for carrying out your trust instructions. Trustees are, of course, entitled to any actual expenses they incur, but also may have to take time off work to meet with accountants or real estate agents or to do other trust-related business. Allotting a set amount of money as a trustee fee on top of whatever the trustee may inherit is not at all unusual and is, I think, appropriate. The amount will depend, of course, on the level of work involved. If the trustee is merely going to wrap up your estate, pay the bills, and hand out the money, a lump sum trustee fee appropriate to the size of the estate would be determined.

However, if the trustee is to continue to act as trustee in years to come to care for the trust fund of a minor or disabled person, an annual fee should be allocated. Keep in mind that a trustee fee is taxable income to the trustee, whereas if you left the trustee a share of the trust as an heir, it would not be considered income, so a share of the estate is more valuable than an equivalent amount of money as a fee.

BACK-UP TRUSTEES

What if your selected trustee cannot or will not act as trustee when the time comes? It is always a good idea to have a second and even a third alternate trustee named in your documents.

Just because you have named someone to be your trustee or executor does not mean they are obligated to do it. A few years ago a woman came to me to represent the estate of her neighbor. The woman had been named by the neighbor as the executor of the will. The estate was not large and the deceased had several children in other states, none of whom liked her. After discussing the probate process with her, I could see she was not happy with the prospect of the big job ahead of her. Finally, I told her she did not have to do it.

She was surprised, having assumed that she had no choice. "Let one of the children be the executor." I said. The will had no back-up named, so the children would either have to agree on one or have the judge appoint someone. She left the papers with me and very cheerfully said she would call one of the sons to tell him her decision.

In your trust, there should be language that provides a mechanism for choosing an alternative trustee if there is none named who is able to do the job. I suggest allowing the beneficiaries to elect a trustee if you can't come up with one, with the guardians of child beneficiaries voting for them. There may be other requirements if the trustee will be enforcing restrictions on when and how a beneficiary receives his share of the trust. You cannot have a trustee in charge of his own restrictions especially in a special-needs trust situation.

WHO CANNOT BE A TRUSTEE

A beneficiary of a special-needs trust cannot be the sole trustee of that trust. The reason is that in a special-needs trust the trustee has the discretionary authority to make whatever distributions the trustee deems appropriate for the beneficiary, provided that benefit programs are not reduced by the distribution. A special-needs beneficiary may end up being disqualified because of the assumed ability to exercise trustee discretion in favor of the beneficiary.

A trustee must be of legal age, mentally competent, should be a resident of the United States, and not a ward of the state under a guardianship order. It helps if the chosen trustee has a good business head and is well organized. Check with your attorney to see if there are special restrictions in your state. A bond is not normally necessary, but if it is the trustee has to qualify for the bond.

A bond is a type of insurance policy that covers any losses to the estate due to the misfeasance or malfeasance of the person bonded. Bonds are only given to bondable people—that is, those who have no criminal history or past conduct that would make them a possible risk to the insurance company. So if the conservator of a person's money runs off with it, the bonding company makes good the loss, then goes after the conservator.

CHAPTER SEVEN

Making Your Trust Work: Funding

Having a trust is a great thing for many reasons as we have discussed, but one of the main advantages is avoidance of probate. In order to avoid probate, all assets above the probate exemption threshold must either be in the name of the trust at the time of death or pass to the trust at that time by way of beneficiary designation.

In my law practice it is not unusual to see clients die who had a trust that was not fully "funded" at the time of their death. Funding is just a word to describe the process of transferring assets to the trust. Any assets left out of the trust will have to go through probate to get into the trust (see the pour-over will in chapter 11).

In some cases there is a trust but no assets at all in the name of the trust—a trust may be fully funded, partially funded, or unfunded. We strive for a fully funded trust to get the probate avoidance advantage.

Everything does not have to go to the trust. As stated earlier, the trust only controls the assets it owns or that pass to it at the death of the grantor. Sometimes a grantor will leave a particular asset such as a bank account or insurance policy to a person outside of the trust by way of beneficiary designation or joint ownership. This is often the case in a blended family where one spouse will leave an asset to his separate children, with the balance of all the trust assets going to all of the children of both spouses. The general rule, though, is that all assets should either be in the name of the trust, pass to the trust at death, or pass to someone else at death. Nothing should have to be probated.

FUNDING METHODS

Funding is not particularly difficult for most assets. Here is a list of common assets and how they are typically funded into a trust.

REAL ESTATE

Real estate is transferred to a trust by way of a deed in most cases. The deed is made from the owner of the real estate to the trustee as trustee of the trust. The deed may be deeded from the grantor to the trust as follows:

"John Smith as trustee of the John Smith Revocable Trust dated January 2, 2010."

There are two kinds of deeds commonly used.

The "warranty deed" is the kind normally provided to the buyer of real estate by the seller. As its name implies, a warranty deed is used to guarantee that the title to the property being sold is genuine and without any encumbrances.

The "quit claim deed" is most often used by attorneys working with trusts. This deed does not guarantee title to the property but merely says that what is being transferred is all the rights to the property owned by the owner of the property. For transfers into trusts, we do not have to worry about guaranteeing title, so a quit claim deed works fine and, in some jurisdictions, is less expensive to file.

In either case the grantor can either record the deed immediately or deliver it to the trustee to be recorded after the death of the grantor. Attorneys are not in agreement as to whether the deed to the trust should be recorded immediately or later, upon the death of the grantor. The advantage of recording is that the deed cannot be lost and you will know it is in proper recordable form. There are states that say that an unrecorded deed is not valid, cannot be recorded after the death of the grantor, and has not effectively been completed until recording. This is another thing to ask your lawyer.

Recording a deed right away may result in additional paperwork if the grantor decides to sell or refinance the property. There may also be reasons not to record it in scenarios involving bankruptcy or qualification for Medicaid for nursing home or other medical care. Should you buy other real estate in the future, be sure it is deeded to the trust. Timeshares in vacation property can be put into the trust name. Real estate located in other states may also be put in the name of your trust, thereby avoiding probate in those other states. Property you are buying on a land contract or contract for deed, where you are not given a deed until the property is paid off, is transferred to the trust by way of an assignment form.

Recording a deed makes it public record, which means that anyone who looks can find out that you have a trust. Recording a deed may also affect certain property tax issues such as homestead rights and may result in removing caps on property assessments. Recording fees may also be high in some states. There are often exemptions available for transfers into a person's revocable trust, so be sure to ask the local tax assessor or your attorney.

Also ask your attorney about potential problems with real estate insurance and title insurance if real estate is in the name of the trust.

BANK AND CREDIT UNION ACCOUNTS

Bank accounts can either be put into the name of the trust directly or, in most institutions, have the trust named as either a co-owner of an existing account or a beneficiary of the account.

The bank may not use the word beneficiary, may call it a "pay on death" (POD) or "transfer on death" (TOD) designation, but it amounts to the same thing. As trust owners, we do not care how the bank or institution does it, so long as at our deaths the money ends up in the trust without probate.

To accomplish the transfer, you need only take your trust certificate (sometimes called the trust abstract) to the bank, where they will copy it and have you sign the appropriate paperwork to make the transfer. You will find that they have had experience with trusts and will guide you on how they handle these accounts at their bank. They may even use a shortened version of the trust name to fit their system. This is okay.

Other bank-type deposit accounts such as certificates of deposit and money market funds can be handled the same way.

STOCKS, BROKERAGE ACCOUNTS

These can also be put directly in the name of the trust, though the transfer process for stocks not being handled by a broker can be trickier. For broker accounts, we send them your trust certificate and they provide the necessary paperwork to either change the account name or put into effect a TOD or POD. This should not be a transaction for which you are charged a fee since it is not a sale or purchase of securities. It is also not a taxable event for capital gains tax purposes.

Stocks that are not being managed in street name or held by your broker are easily identified, since you will have an actual paper stock certificate issued by the corporation and sent to you. Transferring these to your trust requires that you contact the stock office of the corporation and ask for the appropriate paperwork. In most cases, the forms must then be counter-signed at your bank or broker with a "medallion signature guarantee," which is something like a fancy notary. After receiving the signed forms and the old certificates, the corporation issues new stock certificates to your trust.

Stock in a "closely held" corporation may only be transferred to your trust if the corporation's by laws allow it. A closely held corporation is one in which the stock is not publicly traded.

Stock in "sub-chapter S" corporations may be held in trust but only while the grantor (maker) of the trust is alive. At his death, the trust must distribute the stock to qualified beneficiaries or divest itself of it within a certain period of time or the corporation risks losing its special tax status.

Online brokerage accounts, such as E-Trade, AmeriTrade, ScottTrade, and others can also be in the name of your trust. In most cases you can download the forms and instructions from their Web sites. They will ask that a copy of the trust certificate be sent to them along with the forms, which may have to be notarized.

As for retirement accounts, Keoghs, IRAs, and 401(k)s, be aware that a transfer of such accounts to a living trust may be considered a taxable distribution of deferred income; therefore, *these should not be put in the name of the trust* but should have the trust named as the *contingent beneficiary* of these accounts with the spouse being the primary beneficiary. This is so that upon the death of one spouse the other retains easier rollover elections. A beneficiary change form and instructions are usually available from the plan administrator.

Government bonds and savings bonds can be transferred to trust ownership through your local bank. The bonds are turned in (not redeemed) to the government, and new bonds are issued in the trust name.

Your local bank can provide you with a form PD 1851 to fill out and transfer savings bonds to the name of the trust.

Titled assets such as vehicles, trailers, boats, and motorhomes can be put into trust ownership by having the title changed at the local Secretary of State or state tax office (or whatever the name is for the state agency issuing titles). In some cases this is not necessary. In Michigan, for example, if a person dies who owns a vehicle in her own name and whose will is not going through probate, the "next of kin," typically a spouse or child, can have title transferred into his or her name directly without any court process merely by presenting the title and death certificate. This process works provided that the total value of the vehicles does not exceed $60,000 or for boats, $100,000. Relying on this method would not be appropriate for blended families since whose children get the vehicles depend upon which spouse died last.

Be sure to talk to your accountant about the tax effect of putting a vehicle in the name of your trust and to your insurance agent to be sure the vehicle is still insured if the trust is the owner.

OTHER ASSETS AND UNUSUAL SITUATIONS

There are some assets that are difficult or even impossible to put into your trust.

Royalties are rights to percentages of profits and can be available for a variety of things. Book royalties will be paid to an author for as long as a book is in publication. Assigning these to a trust will require the permission of the publisher, and I have seen publishers refuse to agree to the assignment. This creates a situation where the estate of the author must deal with royalty checks for years after the rest of the estate has been settled and closed.

Royalties on oil or gas leases are paid for a fixed period of time according to the terms of the original written lease and are typically assignable to a trust. Other royalties on things such as patents, trademarks, copyrights, profit percentages on films, songs, software programs, and business contractual arrangements may or may not be assignable, depending upon the contract that was signed. In my office we assign these to the trust even if we are not sure, because it costs nothing if we are wrong but is a great advantage if we are right.

CELEBRITY IMAGES

We have all heard that Elvis makes more money now than he did when he was alive. The royalties received by his estate were not assigned to a trust so far as I know, but could have been. Celebrity images and the use of a name are intangibles that can be assigned to a trust.

Animals with pedigree papers can be placed in trust ownership. Thoroughbred horses, show dogs, and even cats can be registered in the name of your trust. Animals with no pedigree can be made part of the trust assets by using the General Assignment of Assets form, which should be included with every trust. Animals, even your favorite pet dog, are considered personal property by the law, no different from your furniture, and so can be listed in the trust on your "Exhibit A" to specify who should receive them.

As an aside, pet trusts are now legal in many states, including Michigan. These are trusts set up to care for the pets by providing a specific dollar amount to be held in trust under the control of a trustee, who pays for the pets' expenses and even pays someone to take care of them.

Aircraft can be placed directly in trust ownership, provided the FAA rules are followed. These are very complex. An Aircraft Registration Application form (AC 8050-1) must be filled out and submitted with a copy of the trust document and a special affidavit containing specific detailed information. I have had aircraft owners who worked for the FAA tell me that it is nearly impossible to get trust ownership of an aircraft through the bureaucracy. There are a few ways to get around this. A corporation can be created to take ownership of the aircraft and the corporate stock placed in the trust name (using a limited liability company works the same way). Another method is to use joint ownership, presumably with someone younger, to have more than just the original owner's name on the registration.

Contract rights may not be assignable to the trust because the assignment is specifically prohibited. For example, interests in a partnership, a real estate cooperative, or even a small corporation or LLC may have such restrictive provisions. The reasoning is that the co-owners do not want to be stuck with the heirs of the trust grantor as partners after the grantor dies. These types of agreements will have buy-sell agreements or provisions regarding the death of a member if they are well drafted.

INSTRUCTIONS TO YOU AS THE GRANTOR AND TRUSTEE

Operation of your trust is quite simple.

TAXES

There are no separate tax numbers necessary (see Employer Identification Number in the glossary). You file your taxes just as you always have in the past without reference to the trust. There is no trust tax return required unless, at the death of a grantor, the trustee is to take over and continue for the benefit of a trust beneficiary.

BANKING

Once your bank and credit union accounts are either in the name of the trust or have a pay-on-death designation filed for them, you do nothing different from what you did before. Your checks do not have to have the name of the trust imprinted upon them, even though the account is in the name of the trust. You do not have to write the word "trustee" after your signature. See the section on accommodation signatures below if you want to give someone else the permission to use the account on your behalf.

REAL ESTATE

The sale or mortgage of real estate operates in exactly the same fashion as before, except if the deed to the trust has been recorded, the name of the seller is the trust and you sign as trustee. The buyer or his title company may require an affidavit from you stating that the trust is still in operation and that you have the authority to sell the property. Upon your death, the successor trustee can immediately assign the property of the trust to the heirs as you have instructed (after paying all your debts, taxes, and other expenses, of course). No probate court directives are necessary. The death certificate is normally recorded with the county deeds records.

NEWLY ACQUIRED ASSETS

Don't forget as time goes by that you have a trust. If you buy new real estate, get a deed made to the trust for the new property. Do the same when opening new accounts or acquiring any new titled assets. These must be funded to the trust in order to keep them out of probate. The pour-over will, described previously, will guarantee that these new assets end up in the trust after the pour-over will is probated, but probate avoidance is a major benefit of your trust and it is up to you to see that the trust stays funded.

CHANGING YOUR MIND

Trusts are easily changed. Much more easily, in fact, than wills. To change a will, you need to sign a codicil. This is a written amendment to the will that must be signed with the same statutory formality of the will itself, which may mean having two disinterested witnesses and in some cases a notary. Changing a trust in most states can be done merely by signing a dated, written statement explaining what you are changing. In some states the trust amendment does not even have to be witnessed or notarized, though as a way of avoiding a fight over whether you actually signed the document or whether you were competent when you did it, I recommend having witnesses and notarizing.

The point is that the trust is revocable, which means it is changeable so long as you are mentally competent.

REVOKING THE TRUST

Usually we do not want to revoke the trust since we want the benefits a trust can provide. Amending it for changed circumstances usually works; however, there are situations where you no longer want the trust.

DEATH, DIVORCE, AND REMARRIAGE

The joint trust that you had with you ex-spouse will likely have to be revoked and redone as an individual trust. The reason is that you were both probably named as co-trustees during your lifetime and each other's trustee upon death or disability. The distribution plans of each of you are likely different than when you were married. The old trust must be "defunded" and the assets placed either in your individual names or the names of your new individual trusts.

Defunding just means taking the assets out of the trust name. While you can sign a document that says the old trust is officially revoked, that is not necessary unless the trust is registered with a court. The trust ceases to exist for all intents and purposes when it has nothing left in its name and nothing is to pass to it on anyone's death.

If you were single when you made the trust and are now married, you will want to talk to your lawyer about how this affects the trust. In community property states (most of the western states plus Wisconsin), you may have to either make a new trust or have your new spouse sign off on your trust plan. A spouse may automatically accede to rights in your trust property by virtue of the marriage. In any event, you will probably want to amend the trust to provide for the new wife or husband. Typical provisions may include use or ownership of the marital home if you die first.

CHAPTER EIGHT

You Do Not Need a Trust If . . .

I know I stated earlier that nearly everyone needs a trust for one reason or another, but in certain very limited situations a trust may not be needed for some people. Sometimes cost is a concern since having an attorney prepare a trust can cost much more than will preparation and you may just not be able to afford the trust.

ALTERNATIVES TO WILLS AND TRUSTS

I typically prepare a handful of wills each year and hundreds of trusts. Sometimes I send potential clients away with neither. Below are some examples of reasons why.

NO ASSETS

A person who owns no real estate or investments often will not go through probate, so probate avoidance would not be a reason to have a trust. Bank accounts can have co-owners on them or in some cases, beneficiaries (sometimes called pay-on-death designees). If a person wants his limited assets to be given to particular people with no strings attached, assuming the people to whom the assets are to be given are adults not suffering from any disability, a beneficiary or co-owner may be all he needs to meet his estate planning needs. (Even those who do not need a trust should still have a durable power of attorney and medical directive—more on this in chapter 11).

Small estates will not have to be probated. In most states there is a threshold below which estates do not have to go through the whole probate process. Usually there is a simplified way to transfer small-sized estates to the beneficiaries. It may be by use of a notarized affidavit or by use of short forms filed with the court office.

The threshold varies from state to state. In California, for instance, estates under $100,000 do not have to go through probate. In Michigan, the amount is much lower, based on a formula that amounts to $20,000 after the deduction of funeral and burial expenses. There are also other deductions that can be made in specific circumstances—usually for married couples or those with minor children to increase the threshold amount. These may be called spousal allowances, homestead allowances, exempt property, or names, but the idea is that you may not have to go through full-blown probate, depending upon the nature and amount of the assets of the deceased.

BENEFICIARY DESIGNATIONS

Beneficiary designations can be a way of avoiding probate if there are no other probatable assets. Probatable assets are those that must go through the probate process in order to transfer title to them to the heirs who are supposed to receive them. Some assets, though, are not subject to probate, because there is another way of transferring them. Joint ownership, described in the next section, is one way, and beneficiary designations are another. Keep in mind that a personal trust may be designated as a beneficiary of an account as described in chapter 7.

Examples of assets that may be transferred by way of a beneficiary designation follow.

Life Insurance. Everyone knows that life insurance is left to the policy owner's survivors by way of a written beneficiary designation. The beneficiary then is the person who receives the life insurance payoff at the insured's death. Suppose there is no named beneficiary who survives the insured. In most cases the "estate" of the insured receives the death benefit.

"Estate of the insured" refers to the probate estate of the insured. So probate is necessary in this case to cash the check for the life insurance, provided that it exceeds the probate threshold in the state of residence of the deceased.

Insurance policy provisions can change this result by setting up default beneficiaries in the event a beneficiary dies. For example, the policy may provide that the money goes to the insured's next of kin. Talk to the lawyer.

If the deceased had a trust, then the trust would be named as the beneficiary. If not, then individuals would be named to get the death benefits. It is possible to leave beneficiaries different shares of a life insurance policy. For example, you may say your son is to get 40 percent of the life insurance as a beneficiary and your daughter to receive 60 percent. Beneficiaries do not have to be treated equally.

Retirement Accounts. Tax deferred accounts come in many flavors, such as IRAs, 401(k)s, 403(b)s, SEP accounts, tax deferred annuities, and many more. All of these can be left to an heir by naming that person as the beneficiary of the account. The beneficiary then steps into your shoes in a way, since he has the ability most of the time to make his own elections as to when and how much to withdraw from the account.

Joint Ownership. One of the traditional ways of avoiding probate, often recommended by lawyers, was to add someone's name on an account or a parcel of real estate. At the death of the original owner, all that had to be shown was the death certificate, and the property belonged to the survivor. It does work to avoid probate. Unfortunately, joint ownership, if not set up correctly, can lead to unanticipated problems. For example, putting someone else's name on your property can mean that you now need the co-owner's permission (and in some states if he is married, his wife's) to mortgage or sell the property. It can also lead to loss of the "stepped-up tax basis" as described in appendix C, causing the new owner expensive capital gains taxes at the time of your death. Merely putting the property in a trust or in a special type of joint deed (such as the ladybird deed explained later in this chapter) gives you the stepped up tax basis at death and minimizes any capital gains tax.

Gifts. Putting someone else's name on your account or property with the intention that they receive it at your death is a gift to them. The gift is subject to federal gift tax laws, and if the value of the gift exceeds the annual exclusion amount ($13,000 at the time of this writing, and which increases annually based on an inflation adjustment), a gift tax return is supposed to be filed to give that information to the IRS. The annual exclusion amount applies to each person to whom you give a gift. No gift tax is due unless the total value of all gifts in excess of the annual exclusions is greater than $1 million during your lifetime.

Also, the making of the gift means that the assets are now assets of the new owner and subject to the claims of the new owner's creditors, including being reachable in bankruptcy proceedings, and may become marital property for divorce property division purposes.

TAX BASIS

The whole area of tax basis, carryover tax basis, and stepped-up tax basis (covered in appendix C) is in flux right now. Under current law, making a gift of property to a person by putting his name on it as a way of avoiding probate may result in a much lower tax basis for that person (meaning higher capital gains taxes) than would putting it into a trust where he could elect to get a stepped-up tax basis (meaning lower capital gains taxes).

LOSS OF CONTROL

Once you put someone's name on your real estate, you now need his permission (and the permission of the wife of a male co-owner in most states) to sell, mortgage, or give away the property. Most people do not want to give up the control of their own real estate.

PROBATE NOT AVOIDED

Probate is not avoided, it is merely postponed. While probate is avoided on the death of one person, at the death of the survivor the property would have to be probated to go to the heirs of the survivor. The survivor would need to make his or her own estate plan to cover this problem.

TRANSFER ON DEATH DEEDS (LADYBIRD DEEDS)

There are people who have very little in assets other than their home and a very simple plan for those assets at death. A full-blown trust-based estate plan may be too expensive for them. In those situations there is a simple alternative. It does involve a type of joint deed, which I have just warned about, but by setting it up properly, you can avoid most of the pitfalls of joint deeds and still avoids probate. This type of deed is sometimes called a "ladybird deed" after the former first lady, wife of President Lyndon B. Johnson, part of whose estate was handled in this manner.

The deed says that the grantor of the property is adding one or more names to the deed, but until the grantor's death, she still retains the right to sell, mortgage, or transfer the property without the permission of the new people. In effect, a gift is made, but it is a contingent gift (what lawyers call a gift of a future interest), which may or may not come to fruition. If the grantor sells the property, the interests of the newly added people are revoked. Because the gift is contingent, the new people cannot exercise any rights of ownership, the property is not reachable by their creditors, and the grantor does not need their permission to mortgage or sell the property. It becomes like a mini-trust.

Some attorneys are now drafting the ladybird deed even for people with regular trusts, naming the trust as the contingent joint owner in answer to some court decisions that put into question the availability of title insurance for trust property or of Medicaid qualification. Medicaid is the federal program providing medical care for indigents. It is administered by the states and each state has its own requirements for qualifying for this benefit. The common requirements are meeting certain minimum asset and income limitations. So a person who does not qualify because she exceeds the asset threshold may be able to change the ownership status of some of the assets to fit into the program.

The rest of the assets of the grantor should either be handled with beneficiary or transfer-on-death provisions, or may be small enough in value to fall below the threshold for requiring formal probate in that state, thereby qualifying for an expedited or affidavit probate process.

The grantor still should have a durable power of attorney, medical power of attorney, and living will, as explained in chapter 11.

CHAPTER NINE

The Many Types of Trusts

"Trust" is only five letters long, but it is a big word. There are dozens of kinds of trusts, complex and simple, for all sorts of purposes. In this book, we are talking about fairly simple trusts, which the IRS refers to as "revocable grantor trusts" (what we normally call revocable living trusts). Revocable just means changeable. The grantor is the person who owns the trust itself. During the grantor's lifetime he may change or revoke the trust. At his death or disability the trust is unchangeable or irrevocable. I am not going to go into detail describing the many trusts available for lots of different purposes, since this would go beyond my intentions for this book.

Other trusts may be created for avoidance or minimization of estate taxes. There are a lot of kinds of trusts for those purposes which can be complex and require the services of a skilled tax or estate planning attorney. Listing and defining all the variations of these trusts goes beyond the scope and intent of this book. The trusts needed by 95 percent of us are for the following purposes.

Probate avoidance is a common benefit shared by all the trusts we use. While probate does not have to be expensive or time-consuming, in many instances it is just that. As I have stated previously, there is no advantage whatsoever to anyone to have your estate go though probate. The only exception, of course, is the probate attorney, who receives a big fee for handling the estate. With a properly funded trust there should be no need for court or even attorney involvement in your estate after your death.

Management of assets for beneficiaries is an extremely good reason to have a trust and this type of trust is essential for anyone with minor children, disabled beneficiaries who are dependent upon federal or state aid, or spendthrifts who cannot manage their own money effectively. Without this type of asset management trust, the money being inherited would go in a lump sum to the beneficiary, which might cause disastrous consequences.

As discussed in chapter 2, a lump-sum distribution to a child when he reaches adulthood is usually a bad idea. Most parents want their children to have the benefit of their inheritance but would prefer to have someone else assist in managing that money to be sure that it is put to the most beneficial use so that it is not wasted.

Having the money held in trust for the child solves that potential problem. The trust itself is not "funded" until the death of the grantor. At that time the trustee begins managing the money for the beneficiary and follows the trust instructions as to when to make trust distributions, for what purposes, and in what amounts. The rules set up for distributions are varied. Common examples of how people do it are:

Attaining a certain age. All the money is held in trust until the beneficiary reaches age twenty-five, for example. Up until then the trustee may be given the authority to use the money for the beneficiary's health, education, welfare, and general living expenses. I have even seen people set up requirements that a portion of the money is to be held as a retirement account for the beneficiary to be turned over to him at age sixty-two and invested until then, essentially creating a retirement account for someone who might otherwise not have one. There may even be provisions allowing money to be paid out in certain limited instances such as medical emergencies. There also must be a provision saying where the money goes if the beneficiary dies before age sixty-two.

A variation on this is giving installments upon the beneficiary attaining different age levels, such as one-third at twenty-five, one-half the balance at thirty, and the remaining balance at thirty-five to split the inheritance into shares so that if a mistake is made with one installment, the beneficiary gets two more shots at it. People often want to split up the inheritance no matter the age of the beneficiary—perhaps one-third at the time of death of grantor, one-half the balance five years later, and the remaining balance ten years after the death of the grantor.

Attaining certain benchmarks. The trust may provide no money to be distributed until the beneficiary does certain things, such as graduating from college, acting as a missionary for a time, or getting married.

JOINT OR INDIVIDUAL TRUSTS FOR COUPLES

Couples can do their estate planning together by having a joint trust, or they may each have their own trust. Which is best depends upon the intentions of the couple, the nature of their assets, and the size of the total asset mix.

For the traditional family unit with a husband, wife, and children (who are the children of both parents) who do not have enough assets to worry about estate taxes (under $3.5 million) and who agree on a plan of asset distribution at both their deaths, a simple joint marital trust is the best answer.

Joint trusts can be made for married couples, gay and other unmarried couples, and even a parent and child. Any two or more people can make a joint trust. Funding a joint trust is easy, since all the grantors put their assets into one trust name—for example, "The John Smith and Mary Doe Revocable Trust." Typical provisions allow both of them to be trustees, and when one dies the survivor continues on in control of all the trust assets without restriction on the ability to use the trust assets and may still have the full right to change the trust terms in any way the survivor desires.

Restrictions can be put into the trust language. For example, there may be a requirement that a survivor cannot change the trust terms in such a way as to disinherit the family of the first trust grantor to die—sort of an anti-disinheritance clause. The terms of the trust may also have different results as to distribution of trust assets, depending upon who is the last to die. So if John is the survivor, the assets would be split one way, and if Mary is the survivor they would be split differently. Often the two grantors will agree on appointing co-successor trustees—one from his side of the family and one from hers.

Individual trusts are most often used for single people who are not in a joint relationship, but not always, as I will explain. The one-person trust has one grantor, and all assets are funded into the name of that trust. The grantor retains all authority over the trust and its assets and controls who gets what and when after he dies.

Married couples often have individual trusts primarily for tax purposes, but also for spousal and family protection.

The traditional estate planning method attorneys have used for married couples with an estate that is potentially subject to estate tax is the so-called "A/B trust." This is really two trusts—a husband trust and a wife trust. The couple's assets are split, with a portion going to one and the rest to the other. At the death of one of the spouses the trust of the deceased is then divided into two portions, an A trust and a B trust. To avoid confusion, we will call the A trust the family trust and the B trust the marital trust.

The survivor usually has some significant restrictions on the use of the assets in the deceased partner's family trust. The income from the family trust is payable to the survivor along with up to 5 percent or $5,000 per year of the principal, whichever is greater. Other than that, the principal itself may not be invaded unless the assets in the survivor's trust are insufficient to maintain the survivor's normal and accustomed standard of living.

At the death of the survivor, both trusts would be distributed to the ultimate beneficiaries named in the trusts. The advantage of this rather cumbersome arrangement is a doubling of the estate tax exemption to avoid estate tax. This is a very necessary objective when the estate tax exemption is low. Estate taxes are charged on the value of an estate that exceeds a minimum threshold. Right now, that amount is quite high at $3.5 million, but seems to change with each president. So for most of us, estate taxes are not a concern. We still sometimes use this method for large estates.

There is a simpler way that utilizes a joint trust to accomplish the same thing. What I call the joint option trust allows all the advantages of the simple joint trust but retains the tax advantages if necessary. This is a good option for couples who agree on an ultimate plan of distribution and who will be the successor trustee. The language of this trust states that at the death of one grantor, the survivor determines whether the current asset size of the joint estate is more than the current estate tax exemption amount. If it is not, the survivor needs to do nothing and has no restrictions on the use of all the trust assets from then on. If it is more, the survivor then allocates the excess taxable portion to a family trust and the balance goes to the marital trust. As we know, there are no restrictions on the marital trust, so this is a great advantage to a surviving grantor.

Single trusts are used by married couples for other reasons. Let's say the wife has a lot of assets that were brought into the marriage and wants to be sure that her husband is cared for during his lifetime. However, she also wants to be sure that at the death of her husband the remaining assets go to her children. She can create a single trust funded with her assets that contains these provisions. She and her husband may also create a separate joint trust for their other assets, and he may have a single trust of his own with similar provisions to hers.

Other kinds of trusts include such things as educational trusts for children, land trusts, and various kinds of charitable trusts which provide income to the grantor for life with the trust going to the charity at death.

CHAPTER TEN

Problems with Trusts

Trusts are not a panacea. That is, there can be problems associated with using trust as an estate settlement method. Trust is the primary problem. Your trustee has to be trustworthy. Since there is no oversight by a court or anyone else, the trustee is the one responsible for making good decisions—investment decisions, financial management decisions, and so forth.

For example, in a down stock market it may be wise to hold stocks for a period of time rather than selling to protect the value of the trust principal. Timing of the sale of assets is a financial management decision. Selecting which assets in which to invest trust funds is a critical decision. Trustees are supposed to be conservative and, absent instructions to the contrary, are supposed to diversify the trust investments. Certainly we would not want to choose a trustee who might invest all the funds in Enron stock.

But because there is no oversight, the only ones the trustee has to report to are the trust beneficiaries, and then only after the fact. The trustee is required to keep good records and keep the trust beneficiaries informed as to trust income and expenses. Unfortunately, by the time the beneficiaries find out about a mistake, the money may already be gone with no way to recover it.

How do we remedy this potential problem? There are four ways:

1. Find a very reliable trustee who will not make these mistakes and who will act honestly. This is a judgment call at best. Most of the time trustees do act honestly and competently and there are no problems. Do not take the warnings here as any indication that trustee abuse is widespread, because it is actually quite rare.

2. Use co-trustees. When more than one trustee is responsible for trust management, there is less likelihood of sloppy bookkeeping, poor asset management, or a trustee embezzling the trust funds.

3. Use an institutional trustee. Banks and trust companies are in the business of acting as trustees and managing trust funds. Their fees typically are about 1 percent of the trust assets per year, but they often can make that up in higher earnings than an individual trustee investor can achieve.

4. Register the trust with the court. Most courts have procedures that allow a trust to be supervised by the local probate court. While this may be more trouble for the trustee and may incur annual attorney fees, it is a way of insuring as best we can that the trust instructions will be carried out and that the trust assets will be preserved. Generally, we do not want court oversight because of the additional

paperwork and bureaucracy attendant, but if you are unsure of your trustee's likelihood of acting in the best interests of your estate, you may want to go for it.

THE TRUST PROTECTOR

The Uniform Trust Act, which is currently in force or pending in a couple dozen states, provides potential protection for trust beneficiaries from a wayward trustee or from changes in circumstance. The act allows the grantors of the trust to appoint a third party or a committee of outside people to supervise the trustee.

The protector's role is set out in the language of the trust document. The protector may be given limited rights to be sure that the intent of the grantors is carried out. These powers may include the right to change the trustee, to change the terms of the trust, or even to add beneficiaries under certain conditions. The rights of the protector are limited to what is given to him in the trust. The purpose is first to be sure the trustee is doing what is supposed to be done. The second purpose is to be sure that if unexpected changes occur the trust is still going to do what was intended. For example, the trust may provide for a share of the trust assets to be given to the five grandchildren of the grantors. Perhaps at the time the trust was made there was no likelihood that there would be any more grandchildren. Then—surprise—another one is born. The protector may be given the ability to add the new grandchild as a beneficiary even if the grantors are long dead.

Or maybe the trustee is just not doing the job properly. Rather than having to go through the probate court to have the trustee replaced, the protector could be given the right to have the trustee replaced. This saves time and money for the beneficiaries.

Or there may be a change in the tax laws that would benefit the trust estate if the trust language could be changed. The
protector could do that.

Family members and beneficiaries should not be the protector, though they may be considered as a committee the protector
consults before making a change in the trust. Typically, the
protector would be the family accountant, a trusted financial
advisor, or other disinterested non-beneficiary third party.

This is not a role that should be put in every trust. In most
cases the trust provisions provide for a complete distribution
of trust assets soon after death. In continuing trusts, though,
a protector may be advantageous to cover the ongoing events
and life changes that may present themselves. Also, keep in
mind that you are adding another layer of complexity to the
trust process by having a protector, and that this is a paying
position. A protector could be a pricey position to create if it is
not strictly needed.

Actually, it is not necessary for the Uniform Trust Act to
be enacted in your state for you to have a protector. Trusts are
so flexible that you can add the specific language to create this
position even without the act. Just be careful putting it in if it is
not needed since this means there is someone looking over the
shoulder of the trustee at all times and may add significant cost
and delay to the trust settlement process.

TRUSTS AND CREDITORS

A revocable trust does not provide asset protection. There are
seminars and courses offered that promote the use of trusts as
a way of protecting your assets from your creditors. Most of
these involve the use of either irrevocable trusts or offshore
trusts with foreign trustees and are sold for big prices by those
running the seminars. In some cases these techniques work, but
sometimes they can be disastrous, and the trust owner finds
himself prosecuted for fraudulent transfers or income tax eva-
sion. Be very careful and get independent legal advice before

using any of these types of trusts. Similarly, having your assets in a revocable trust does not guarantee that you will qualify for Medicaid benefits for nursing home care. The asset and income limitations still apply, and trust assets are considered as your assets for qualification purposes.

The purpose of the revocable living trust is not creditor protection. The trust described in this book has as its purposes: probate avoidance, asset management, and estate tax minimization, but not protection from creditors or lawsuits.

GUARDIAN AND TRUSTEE ARE TWO DIFFERENT ROLES

One problem we occasionally see is when the guardian of minor children is also named as the trustee of their trust fund money. This is an inherent conflict of interest since the guardian would be the one asking the trustee for funds for the care of the children. It sounds okay but can lead to abuses.

An example: Mom and Dad died, leaving three young children as survivors. A friend of the family was named as their trustee and guardian. The trustee had children of her own and made a decision to use the trust funds to add onto her house to provide a playroom for all the children. While this decision temporarily benefited the children, in the long run it benefited the trustee, since the money added to the value of her home. (She had to give the money back.)

Had the trustee and guardian roles been separated, it is unlikely the trustee would have agreed to the building of the playroom.

WHY YOU MAY NOT WANT A JOINT TRUST

A joint trust between two or more people normally will have their joint and individual assets funded into it. Then there is one set of instructions that tell the trustee what to do with those assets at one or both deaths. The first thing that is done after identifying the assets is paying the debts. That can be a problem.

If one partner has a lot of debt that is not jointly owed by the other partner, the amount of the individual debt will have to be paid from the joint trust assets at the death of the debtor. This can be disastrous to the surviving grantor.

I had a client whose husband, who was seriously ill, owed over $100,000 resulting from a lawsuit over a failed business venture. At his death, the joint trust would have been responsible for the entire debt, even though most of the assets belonged to the wife before the marriage. Fortunately, before he died, we were able to revoke the joint trust, remove her assets, and set up an individual trust for her. When he died, only his separate assets were liable for the debt, so the wife's assets were preserved. Analyze the respective debts of the two grantors to see if this could be an issue.

CHAPTER ELEVEN

Guardians, Powers of Attorney, and More

All states allow a parent to nominate the guardian who will take over the raising of children at the death of the parents. If you are divorced, the surviving parent will typically become the custodian automatically, but we recommend naming a guardian anyway, just in case the other parent is unable or unwilling to act as guardian.

GUARDIANSHIP OF CHILDREN

The guardian is the person who takes the place of the parent in raising the child. This person will also be the Social Security payee for survivor's benefits. The conservator is the person who handles the child's money that may not be part of the child's trust funds and is supervised by the courts.

Naming a guardian is typically done by language in a will, though in some states it can also be done by affidavit. The statement is simple, merely stating something like this: "I nominate and appoint Mary Doe of 123 Maple Street, Detroit, Michigan,

as guardian of my minor children." Nothing fancy or complicated, but legally sufficient when signed and witnessed in a
properly drafted will.

Usually we name the person as "Conservator" of the children's money as well, though if the guardian is not the trustee
of the children's money, we would name the trustee as the
conservator.

But isn't the point of this book to use trusts and not wills?
Yes. However, in every trust-based estate plan there is still a
will, though it is rarely used to transfer assets and is usually not
probated because the trust takes care of all that. The will does
have another use.

The will is one way to name a guardian and conservator for
your children even if it is not formally probated.

GUARDIANSHIP OF ADULTS

There is a whole section of the court system devoted to adult
guardianship. Adults have accidents and strokes, develop
Alzheimer's disease and dementia, or have physical conditions
that render them unable to care for themselves. If proper planning has not been done, the person's family is forced to petition
the court for guardianship and conservatorship in order to care
for the person.

Court-supervised guardianship and conservatorship is a
burdensome problem for the family. While the purpose is to
be sure that the person and his finances are properly cared
for, the court oversight and reporting requirements are a lot
to put family members through. The court hearings, which
are periodically required, may take most of a day and typically involve just waiting for your turn in front of the judge.
Attorney fees are often required, as are court costs and a
court-appointed guardian ad litem (a court-appointed person who is watching out for the interests of the person who
needs the guardianship, usually an attorney), who charges
the estate as well.

To avoid the court-ordered adult guardianship, all you have to have are two documents in addition to the trust itself. These are part of every well-drawn estate plan.

DURABLE POWER OF ATTORNEY

Durable power of attorney is a permission slip entitling someone else to legally sign your name. It gives them the right to sign documents with the same authority and legal effect as if you had signed them yourself. Deeds, checks, tax returns, and any other document that you authorize can be signed by the person who has your power of attorney, who is, in effect, your agent. Thus, your agent can pay your bills for you and do your business without getting permission from the courts. (Lawyers sometimes call your agent your "attorney-in-fact" even though these agents are not necessarily attorneys.)

There are two basic kinds of powers of attorney: immediate and springing. An immediate power of attorney is effective, valid, and usable the moment it is signed. We use this for those who want someone to help them pay their bills and manage things for them because they need the help right now. Maybe they can do it themselves, but it is more convenient to have someone's help. A son or daughter may run to the bank for an elderly parent who has physical limitations, for example, even though mentally the parent has no diminished capacity.

A springing power of attorney only goes into effect if a certain condition is met. Typically this might be if two physicians certify in writing that the person is incapable, due to physical or mental incapacity, of making reasoned decisions regarding his financial affairs. This is the kind most younger people want since they are healthy and do not want someone else to have the broad authority over their accounts and assets.

The danger of a power of attorney is that it can be misused. Since the agent can sign your name, she can do anything you can do, including sell your real estate, empty your bank accounts, and even borrow money on your credit. Be very careful to whom you give this power.

Power of attorney may be limited as to time or may be limited in scope. It may be convenient to have someone sit in for you on a real estate closing while you attend to other business. That person can sign all the necessary paperwork and receive the sale proceeds with a power of attorney. This type of document could be written to specifically limit the power of attorney to that one transaction, for a limited time period, and then the power of attorney would automatically expire.

In the estate planning area, we typically use very broad powers of attorney. The only restriction is that the agent, in most cases, cannot create or modify a person's will or trust.

Power of attorney can be revoked at any time by the maker by notifying the agent in writing. If this happens, it is a good idea to also contact any financial institutions that the agent may have dealt with to let them know of the revocation of authority and supply them with a new document containing the new agent's name.

One caveat: Sometimes powers of attorney will not be honored even if properly drawn up. While these are legal documents, there is no law at this time in most states that requires a financial institution or anyone else to recognize the authority of the agent. Not honoring power of attorney is rare, but it does happen and there is no way to force the issue. Legislation has been drafted to overcome this problem, but in most states the problem exists.

MEDICAL POWER OF ATTORNEY

This is the second document needed to protect against court-ordered adult guardianship. Similar to the durable general power of attorney, the medical power of attorney grants to some other person the right to make medical decisions for you if you cannot make them for yourself. This decision-making authority is for such things as consenting to surgery and medical procedures, but also extends to decisions on termination or continuation of life support, so picking the person with this power is a serious decision. You should also consider whether the person you are naming is emotionally capable of acting in this capacity. Terminating life support is a heavy burden, and some people just cannot do it, even if that is what the patient wants.

If you have a revocable trust, a durable power of attorney, and a medical power of attorney, it is unlikely that a judge would bother appointing a guardian or conservator, since you have all the help you need in the event of disability. Some of the petitions to appoint a guardian and conservator—the court-promulgated documents—even ask the question of whether such documents already exist.

LIVING WILL

If someone is going to make medical decisions for you, he or she will want to know what decisions to make. The living will (which is not a will at all) is a document you sign in which you state your wishes as to the use of life support, feeding tubes, organ donation, medical procedures, and such. While not a legally binding document in most states, it is a good thing to have since it avoids any disagreement among family members as to what you would have wanted done in particular situations if you are unable to tell them yourself.

PERSONAL PROPERTY DESIGNATIONS

In a good trust, there will be an addendum (which is just a blank page at the end of your trust, sometimes called Exhibit A) on which you can list particular items of personal property and who is to get each item. You do not have to use the form, but if there are special one-of-a-kind items like wedding rings or Grandpa's shotgun, having a signed statement by you as to who is supposed to get those items avoids a lot of misunderstanding among the family.

TRUST CERTIFICATE

This is a document containing a summary of certain parts of your trust language. It may also be called a certificate of trust existence, an abstract of trust, or another title, but the purpose is the same. It is requested by institutions to prove that the trustee has the authority, and the trust has the power, to conduct certain transactions. It may be used by a real estate title insurance company to guarantee that real estate being sold or mortgaged in the trust name is legally sufficient, title-wise. Brokers and bankers may want a copy as evidence of the existence of the trust, its proper name and date, and identification of the trustees and successor trustees. At your death, when your successor trustee shows up at the bank with your death certificate, the banker will know from the trust documents that he is turning over your accounts to the correct person. If you should change successor trustees, be sure to replace the trust certificates at these institutions to reflect the correct names.

CHAPTER TWELVE

Trustee Instructions for
Death or Disability

So now we know why a trust is necessary, what kind of trust to get, how to get it prepared, and how to fund it. But what happens next? What happens to the trust when the trust owner becomes disabled or dies? Most of the information we see about trusts from seminars, news articles, and books explains why a trust is needed and how to go about funding one. There is very little information out there on what to do with the trust at the death of the trust owner.

One of the reasons we recommend a trust over a will is that the trust can provide an automatic manager of the trust assets if the grantor becomes disabled. People with dementia, or who have had strokes or any other disability, will not be able to take care of their financial affairs. Someone has to be able to pay the bills, do the taxes, and manage the money. Without a trust the family would be forced to petition the probate court for the power to take over. As discussed earlier, this is a time-consuming and expensive process. Part of this can be done with power of attorney, but the rules of the trust itself give the second-in-line trustee—the successor trustee—the power to take over, should this situation occur.

Typically the successor trustee would meet with the grantor's doctor and, if appropriate, the social worker at the hospital or nursing home to be sure there is a confirmed diagnosis of disability. A written opinion of the diagnosis is best. This satisfies the trust language, which requires proof of actual disability. Armed with this and the power of attorney, the successor trustee can then contact bankers and investment advisors to assume the financial management role.

Trust settlement is the term used to describe the process of wrapping up the affairs of the grantor after death and carrying out the instructions in the trust as to disposition of the trust assets. Attorneys are very good at trust settlement, and if you do not care about the cost of settling the trust or the amount of time it might take, the easiest way to settle a trust is to hire a lawyer.

The thing is that the work that needs to be done at death is not legal work. It is a mostly clerical job that almost anyone can do if they have some direction. Why pay lawyer rates at hundreds of dollars an hour for things you can easily do yourself? I am going to give you a step-by-step guide on how to settle a trust without a lawyer.

It's true that I do not recommend setting up your trust without a lawyer, but the trust settlement part is entirely different. A lawyer is usually not needed.

As discussed earlier, a trustee is a fiduciary, a person with a special responsibility both to the trust creditors and the trust heirs. If the trustee makes a mistake, he can be personally responsible for making good on it. That's why some trustees go ahead and hire the lawyer—to help cover their liability. If you as a trustee decide to hire a lawyer to help you, make sure she understands that you know the process and plan on doing as much of the work as possible yourself, leaving the lawyer with only lawyerly things to do. Do not let the lawyer talk you into letting him handle all the money and keep the checkbook. You or your accountant can pay the bills and write the checks.

THE SETTLEMENT PROCESS

Settling a trust consists of three steps:

1. Identify and collect the assets.

2. Identify and pay the debts and obligations.

3. Distribute the trust assets as directed in the trust document.

Seems pretty simple, and it is. Of course, there are lots of potential components to each step, but I am going to try to lay out the most common areas you are likely to encounter. If something comes up that is not covered here, you can always pay a trust attorney for a half-hour conference to ask a question or two. (You do not have to turn the trust over to him, though.)

Settlement of a trust after the death of one grantor in a joint trust is usually simple. The assets may stay in the trust under the continuing control and management of the survivor, who just has to take care of cashing in or rolling over beneficiary-type assets, and then nothing happens until the survivor dies. But this is not always the case, so I recommend being careful and looking for the following possible issues.

After the death of the first grantor to die, the survivor should do the following in relation to the trust.

Life Insurance. Contact the life insurance companies and request a claim form. This should then be filled out and returned to them with a certified copy of the death certificate. In most cases the death benefit will be paid within thirty days.

Real Estate. If the real estate has previously been transferred to the joint trust by deed, nothing needs to be done since the trust is still in existence and still owns the real estate. As the surviving partner and surviving trustee, you are in charge of the trust and all trust assets, including the real estate. You may file a certified copy of the death certificate in the county where the property is located, but you are not required to do so at this time, and this may be done by your successor trustee at your death.

Personal Property. If the trust requires that certain personal property items of your partner's be transferred to named beneficiaries now rather than at your death, you, as the survivor, must now transfer those items to those persons.

Income Tax. The tax returns for the year of your spouse's death may be made as "married filing jointly" if you wish, but the last year's income tax return for your spouse must be filed.

Estate Tax. If the property and other assets of the trust, including property passing by beneficiary designation and property in the name of your spouse outside of the trust, exceed the estate tax exemption amount (currently $3,500,000, but subject to change), then you should consult your accountant or attorney about the need for filing a federal estate tax return Form 706. Even if no tax is due now, the filing of a return may still be required. It may also be necessary, if you had, for instance, an A/B trust, to obtain a separate Taxpayer Identification Number for the trust. In the case of an A/B trust, it is also very desirable to get provable valuations in place for all trust assets as of the date of death so that you can prove the values at that time. It can sometimes be difficult to establish a value at death for real estate or a business, for example, a year or two later.

Benefits. Contact the Social Security office to see what survivors benefits may be payable to the surviving spouse or children as well as to apply for the Social Security death benefit. Contact any previous employers to be certain that all employee benefits have been applied for. Form letters are included to initiate this process.

Wrongful Death. If the death was or could have been the result of another person's negligence, such as medical malpractice or an auto accident, contact your attorney to see what benefits may be available for the family.

As was explained earlier, there are two basic types of trusts—the joint trust and the single trust. If you have a joint trust with a spouse, a parent, or a life partner, you should be sure that nothing has to be done at the death of one of you insofar as the trust is concerned. So in a joint trust, this is what might need to be done in some cases.

READ THE TRUST (OR HAVE YOUR ATTORNEY EXPLAIN IT TO YOU)

The language of the trust document itself needs to be reviewed to see what happens to the trust at the death of one of the co-grantors. Most often the trust will say that all the trust assets stay in trust and under the control of the surviving grantor. The survivor can still spend the money, borrow against the assets, sell them, or do anything that was possible before. The trust distribution provisions typically do not take effect until both grantors die. Often the surviving grantor has the ability to change the trust in any way desired. This is not always the case, so read the trust carefully.

There are numerous types of provisions that may take effect immediately upon the first death. Read the trust carefully to be sure you, as the surviving grantor, are doing everything correctly. It may be a good idea to go to the lawyer who prepared the trust to have her review the trust provisions with you. If you are making up your trust now, you may want to include some of these provisions in your trust, if they apply, or to remove the more onerous ones. Here are some examples:

1. Can you change the trust? Often in the case of blended families, the grantors want to be sure that if one of them dies first, the children of the first

to die are not going to be disinherited by the survivor. So the trust may have a provision that the survivor may not change the trust in one or more ways. It becomes, in effect, wholly or partially irrevocable at the death of one. Even if the survivor can't change the beneficiaries, there may still be the power to make limited amendments, such as changing the successor trustees. If the trust is silent as to limitations on the right to amend after the death of one of you, the survivor can change the trust provisions in any way or even revoke the trust altogether.

2. A surviving grantor may discover from reading the document that while he cannot change the trust, he still retains the ability to remove assets from it or to make gifts. To thwart the no-amendment provision, the survivor may remove all the trust assets or give them away to effectively revoke the irrevocable trust. Provisions should be in the trust that prevent this sort of end-run around the rules.

3. There are sometimes family heirlooms or one-of-a-kind items that a grantor may want to see end up in the hands of his own heirs. Often a trust will instruct that these individual items go immediately to the people indicated without waiting for the death of the surviving grantor. Things like collections, jewelry, firearms, sporting goods, the family bible, collector cars, or other such possessions can be listed on an addendum to the trust that must be followed at the death of one person. However, the trust must specifically provide in its language that if such a list is appended to the document, it must be followed.

4. Often the family home is owned by one of the grantors prior to the beginning of the relationship. The plan may be to pass the place on to the next generation after the death of the parent. The other partner may face undue hardship if forced to leave the house and find another place to live. Trusts often provide that the surviving grantor has the right to remain in the home for a set period of time (or for his lifetime), following which the property is given to the ultimate beneficiaries. In the meantime, either the trust pays the expenses on the property or, more commonly, the survivor is responsible for such things as taxes, insurance, maintenance, and utilities.

   Again, if the trust is silent as to the residence, it remains part of the trust principal and belongs to the surviving partner, who can sell it, mortgage it, or even give it away.

   And don't forget about the furniture and household goods. I had a case where the trust provided that the survivor had the right to live in the house but was silent as to the furniture. The children of the deceased grantor, who were the ultimate beneficiaries, removed all of it. So while the survivor had the right to live in the house, he had to buy all new furniture, silverware, pots and pans, and even bath towels. A trust provision could cover that kind of situation.

5. New trustees. To make sure the trust provisions are followed, careful grantors will sometimes provide that at the death of one of them, the surviving grantor is no longer solely in charge of the trust management. Often a bank or one of the deceased grantor's children will be added as a co-trustee along with the surviving grantor.

This is not necessarily a bad thing, since it ensures that the survivor has no choice but to honor the terms of the trust, but it does make for complications on the part of the survivor. From that point on, the survivor has to agree on all financial decisions with the new co-trustee. I had a client whose husband died, and the trust appointed his daughter as the co-trustee with the wife. While the husband was alive, the client thought the plan would work fine, but after he died, the stepdaughter made every effort to conserve all the trust assets, refusing or complicating every request for money from the trust.

Her thinking was that the stepmother was spending the ultimate inheritance. The courts could have intervened to appoint a new trustee, but this would have added another layer of cost and complexity to the process. Adding a trustee to serve along with your partner is a good idea in theory, but in practice it can lead to rather contentious situations. Be careful what provisions are put in the trust, since they are very difficult (if not impossible) to change, and your co-grantor will have to live with them.

6. Changing trust asset management. At the death of one grantor, some trusts will have provisions that put the survivor on what amounts to an allowance. A new trustee is in charge of paying the bills for the surviving partner. The survivor gets her expenses paid for life, but at death, the trust assets pass on to the heirs named in the trust. There is no right to the use of the principal, except in limited amounts and circumstances. These provisions are typically put in for estate tax purposes,

but sometimes to preserve the assets in the trust for the ultimate beneficiaries. When you set up your trust, be sure that you understand the effect these provisions will have on the survivor. Most often the surviving partner resents having limitations on access to what was once jointly owned property.

7. Tax provisions. Years ago, when estate taxes were assessed on estates of $600,000 and up, estate tax provisions were a valuable part of any good trust. Now, the threshold is $3.5 million, so this is not an issue for most people. The problem is that many trusts were created a long time ago and have not been brought up to date to reflect the new laws. Consequently, some surviving grantors find themselves subject to restrictions on their access to the joint trust assets that serve no tax-saving purpose yet severely limit their financial activities.

The "QTIP" provision is a common one. This acronym stands for Qualified Terminable Interest Property. It's a mouthful, and a detailed explanation is beyond the scope and intent of this book. Briefly, this trust provision has been used to avoid estate taxes and is still used for the larger estates that may exceed the $3.5 million threshold.

Here's how it works. Each grantor has today what amounts to a $3.5 million exemption from estate tax. The problem in larger estates is that if one grantor dies before the other, the survivor gets all of the assets tax-free (due to the unlimited marital deduction), but then at the death of the survivor there would be only one estate tax deduction left. So at today's tax rates, a $5-million-dollar estate could end up paying nearly half a million dollars in federal estate taxes. The QTIP provision in a trust could solve that problem by allowing the taxable portion over the exemption amount to be placed in a separate account. The survivor could draw the interest, and in some cases, part of the principal each year from that account, and then at the death of the survivor, the remainder would go to the ultimate beneficiaries. That way the survivor would have one exemption, and the first to die would have his exemption preserved to shield the QTIP amount from estate taxes. In effect, this doubles the estate tax exemption to $7 million, so at death there would be no estate taxes whatsoever.

Sounds good, but some poorly drafted trusts will require that a certain portion of the trust assets be put into a QTIP share, even if there is no tax problem due to the size of the total trust estate. A $2.5-million-dollar estate would have no federal tax liability, yet some trusts will put half of it into the restrictive QTIP anyway. (While it was common years ago for most states to have a separate state inheritance tax, most states now use a so-called pickup tax, which allows them a share of the federal tax collected. A half-dozen states still retain some form of inheritance tax with varying exemption levels. Contact your accountant or use the Internet to look up the rules in your state.)

Another big problem area is the older A/B trusts, sometimes called marital and family trusts. These act very much like the QTIP in that they divide the trust into separate shares, and the spouse gets the marital share without restriction and has limited access to the family share. The older ones sometimes have language requiring that all the trust assets that do not qualify for the marital deduction go to the family trust to preserve an estate tax exemption on taxable estates. However, the marital deduction is now unlimited, which means that under the terms of the trust all the assets would go to the marital trust and there would be no tax savings by preserving the deduction of the first to die.

There are a lot of kinds of trusts, often with very complex provisions that even lawyers have a hard time deciphering. Be sure you completely understand all the provisions that are going to govern your access to your own money before you let a lawyer put them in the document. As discussed earlier, some lawyers may be using form software that already contains the provisions, and they may be in your document whether they are appropriate for your situation or not.

The lesson here is that if you find these complicated tax provisions in the trust you are about to administer, or if you are the surviving grantor, it is wise to see a trust attorney (not just any old attorney) to find out how this affects you and what you need to do. It may be that you will have to immediately begin partial administration of the trust even before the death of the co-grantor because of the need to carry out instructions in the trust that take effect at the death of the first to die.

If both grantors are liable for a debt, such as a mortgage, then the survivor can continue to make any required payments just as before. Most contracts do not have an acceleration clause at the death of one debtor. However, if a grantor dies and the co-grantor is not jointly liable for the debt, it must be paid off in full out of the trust assets. As an example, I have seen cases where only one person has signed on a mortgage who then dies. The survivor has no legal right to continue to make the mortgage payments but must either pay it off or refinance. This is what you might call a due-on-death clause.

So credit cards, auto loans, taxes, and even mortgages in only the name of the deceased are due and payable in full out of trust assets, provided they are not joint debts. If you discover that your partner had debts in her own name, then they must be paid at death from the trust assets, even if those assets were mostly put in the trust by the survivor. This was referenced earlier in this book, and the remedy sometimes is to have separate trusts for each partner.

ADDITIONAL STEPS TO TAKE
WHEN SOMEONE DIES

After the funeral and burial details have been carried out, there are other things that need to be done when a partner dies. The following apply to the death of one grantor of a joint trust, the surviving grantor's death, and the death of a sole grantor of a single-person trust.

1. Order at least a dozen death certificates. It is easier to get several at first than it is to get more later, and they will be needed for various purposes. When you give these out, see if a photocopy will suffice, since a certified death certificate can cost $25 or more. You may need them for life insurance claims, Social Security benefits, VA benefits, probate of the will if necessary, and pension or profit sharing plans, as well as a copy to include with federal or state estate tax returns.

2. Cancel credit cards that were just in the name of the deceased or in the name of his or her business. As a practical matter, even though these should be paid off in full at death, if the card is no longer being used and there is not enough ready cash to pay them, you may be able to get an agreement to continue the payments. You should never use the cards yourself unless you are an authorized signer.

3. Similarly, cancel other services such as debit cards, telephone and cell-phone accounts, Internet services and subscriptions, cable television, and other recurring expenses that are only in the name of the deceased. They may require a copy of a death certificate to process the cancellation.

4. Keep up payments to maintain real estate (such as utilities, taxes, and insurance) until the property can be sold or transferred. We have had incredibly expensive repairs required when the gas and electric were cut off on vacant property and the water pipes froze and broke. The trustee is responsible for managing and preserving the property of the trust and could be held liable for failing to do so.

This would be only for property separately in the name of the deceased. Jointly owned property or property in the joint trust will continue to be under the control and management of the survivor, so the survivor would continue to maintain the trust properties.

FINDING ASSETS

1. Contact employers for information on benefit programs. There may be unpaid vacation pay, the last paycheck, life insurance, retirement accounts, or profit sharing benefits that would accrue to either the trust or the person's family or estate.

2. File claims for life insurance and other death benefit accounts such as annuities. This is a very simple process of filling in a claim form and returning it to the insurance company with a death certificate. The insurance proceeds would be payable to the named beneficiary, which we would hope to be the trust. It may be necessary to open a bank account in the name of the trust in which to deposit the check if you have not already opened one for the joint trust. Remember, too, that some credit card companies offer free life insurance to their cardholders. If there are loans due, find out whether the deceased

had credit life insurance to cover these. The original loan paperwork will usually tell you this.

3. File claims for retirement accounts. Things like IRAs, 401(k)s, 403(b)s, tax-deferred annuities, and myriad other assets have beneficiaries. The claim would be filed on behalf of the beneficiary, and the plan administrator will provide information on what elections are available to the beneficiaries. A spouse as a beneficiary, for example, may be able to roll over the account into an IRA in his or her own name, thereby continuing to defer the tax owed. Filing the claim is just a matter of filling out a form according to its written instructions. The company representative will typically help you with this.

4. If the deceased is a veteran, contact the VA office for what benefits may be available. A form letter is included in the appendix for that purpose.

5. Contact any organizations to which the deceased belonged and see if there are any benefits available. Some of them may have insurance programs for their members. Again, there is a form letter for you to use in the appendix.

6. Try to identify any online accounts the deceased may have had. Sometimes there are substantial assets in accounts through ETrade, ScottTrade, and other online brokerage or banking accounts. There are even online gambling accounts some people have in which they keep deposits. Similarly there may be accounts for commodities, such as money invested in gold funds.

7. Look for refundable deposits with utility companies or landlords.

8. If auto insurance or homeowner insurance is canceled, there may be refunds of unearned premium due to you as the trustee of the estate. It is a good idea to talk to the insurance agent of the deceased, who can help with identifying other assets.

9. Contact banks and credit unions to be sure all accounts are in the name of the joint trust, and, if not, see if they have a "pay on death" designation or a beneficiary naming you or the trust as the owner at death. The bank will want a death certificate. If there are accounts that exist just in the name of the deceased with no beneficiary on them, they must be transferred via the pour-over will to the trust using, ideally, the small estate probate procedure in your state.

10. Identify business interests. If the deceased had business interests such as partnerships, sole proprietorships, LLCs, or corporations, these would typically already be in the name of the trust. If there are others involved, there may be partnership agreements or buy-out agreements, which would pay the estate of the deceased for the share of the business value. Businesses may be continued or sold depending upon the feasibility of either approach and the instructions of the deceased.

11. Search the house. Look through desk drawers and paperwork for evidence of insurance policies, savings bonds, or other assets. I once found a manila envelope on a bookshelf crammed with other paperwork

in the house of a person whose estate I was settling. Inside was a paid-up insurance policy with a cash value of over a quarter million dollars. It was a fluke that I ran across this, but it ended up being a big surprise to the family. It is not unusual for people to hide valuables in their home, though difficult to find sometimes. If there is a family safe, be sure that the successor trustee knows the combination. It is a shame to have to destroy a perfectly good safe to get it open because no one knows how to get into it. Contrary to what you see at the movies, it is not always possible to have some gizmo figure out the combination. The last time I had a safe company assist in opening a safe, they ended up doing it with two big men, a sledgehammer, and a large pry-bar.

12. Though not as commonly used today, some people still have safe deposit boxes at their banks. If the box is in the name of the trust, or if there is another authorized signer, you may be able to access the box without involving the courts simply by presenting the death certificate.

13. The decedent's mail should be forwarded to the trustee. Watch the mail carefully, since you may discover statements sent out quarterly or annually, revealing assets of which you were unaware. Bills will be coming in, too, usually by mail.

VALUING ASSETS

Most assets are easily valued since they will be converted to cash immediately after the death of the deceased. Some assets, though, will be kept intact in a joint trust situation, and a verifiable appraisal may be a valuable tool later on. Real estate, for example, may be part of a potentially taxable estate. The value at date of death may have to be proved to show either the amount of estate tax owed or that a tax return was not needed because the value kept the estate below the threshold for taxation. Valuation, which is provable, is also used to establish a value as of date of death for capital gains tax purposes to establish a new tax basis for the assets.

When assets are to be divided on a percentage basis among several heirs and some things are to be given out individually without liquidating them, we need to be able to prove the value in order to show how much of the person's share who received the asset was represented by it. For example, it is common to have collections, antiques, or other personal property items left to a particular heir with the understanding that the item is to be considered part of her share of the estate. We do not want an argument over the value of the share, and an appraisal solves the problem.

INCOME TAXES

An income tax return must be filed for the deceased for the year of death if there was taxable income. Even if there wasn't any income tax liability, the deceased may have been eligible for certain local, state, or federal tax rebates or credits that could be claimed by filing the return. Also, pay attention to any estimated tax payments that may have been made by the deceased. Always find the deceased's last year income tax return and contact the preparer to see what issues may exist or for help in filing the last return.

If you are the surviving spouse, you may file a joint return for the year of death. Talk to your accountant about the best plan for you.

NOTIFYING EVERYONE

Part of the obligation of the trustee is to notify creditors and heirs of the death and of the existence of the trust.

In a joint trust, the heirs do not need to be notified unless they are to receive something immediately or if the trust document calls for it. The trustee would notify them after both trust grantors are gone.

Notification of heirs is typically done by sending a letter and a copy of the trust to each heir. In some states there is only the obligation to send the portion of the trust that pertains to that particular heir. From then on the heirs must be kept updated on what assets are in the estate and what expenses come out of the estate. This can be done at the time the assets are distributed, unless it drags on for some reason, in which case annual reports should be provided. Good communication lessens complaints to the trustee by heirs.

Notification of creditors is a bit different. In a trust we want to be able to settle matters quickly, without the fear of an unknown creditor presenting a claim after the assets have been distributed to the heirs. In some states this is an easy matter. Michigan, for instance, allows a trustee to publish a notice in the newspaper called a "Notice To Creditors," which lets everyone know that there has been a death and allows any unknown creditors a limited amount of time (in this case, four months) to present their claim before they are forever barred from bringing it up later. This gives the trust a short statute of limitations and allows the trust to be closed up quickly and safely.

Known creditors must be contacted individually either by paying the debts or by sending notice of the death so that they can bill the trust for what is due. It is a good practice to send all doctors, clinics, and hospitals, as well as other health care providers, a copy of the Notice to Known Creditors to put them on notice to get their billings to you or they will not be paid. Hospitals are notorious for sending medical bills months after services are provided.

PAYING THE DEBTS AND EXPENSES

Now the assets are known and the debts are all totaled. If sufficient funds are available, go ahead and pay the debts in full, keeping statements and receipts for your records. If the debts exceed the assets, we have a problem.

State laws set up rules on how claims are to be paid in probate cases if there are insufficient funds, and, in some states, the same rules apply to trusts. These laws refer to "priority of claims." Here is a common set of rules:

If the applicable estate property is insufficient to pay all claims and allowances in full, the personal representative shall make payment in the following order of priority:

(a) Costs and expenses of administration.

(b) Reasonable funeral and burial expenses.

(c) Homestead allowance.

(d) Family allowance.

(e) Exempt property.

(f) Debts and taxes with priority under federal law, including, but not limited to, medical assistance payments that are subject to adjustment or recovery from an estate under section 1917 of the Social Security Act, 42 USC 1396p.

(g) Reasonable and necessary medical and hospital expenses of the decedent's last illness, including a compensation of persons attending the decedent.

(h) Debts and taxes with priority under other laws of this state.

(i) All other claims.

The "all other claims" would then be paid pro rata at so many cents on the dollar after dividing the total remaining assets by the remaining debts to get the ratio.

A point that might help you in a situation with more debts than assets is that the first priority is costs and expenses of administration, which includes the fees of the trustee and/or personal representative. If you are the surviving partner you can charge a fee, usually hourly, for everything you do to settle the estate, the money for which comes off the top. Check state law, of course, to be sure this works where you live, and check the language of the trust, which may spell out what the trustee fees would be. In most cases the debts will not exceed the assets, so everything can be paid in full.

TAX IDENTIFICATION NUMBERS

A Tax Identification Number for a living person is his Social Security Number. That number cannot be used after death, so a Tax Identification Number should be obtained for the trust itself. With that number the trustee may open bank accounts, cash checks payable to the trust, and put in claims for trust assets. It once was a lengthy process to get a Tax ID Number using the IRS Form SS-4. Not anymore. These can be obtained online by going to the IRS Web site and filling out the online form. The number will be provided immediately. Alternatively, you can call a toll-free number or fill out the SS-4 and apply by fax. The IRS calls these Employer Identification Numbers, even though for a trust there is no employer. Here is the contact information, current as of the time this book went to press.

Web site:
www.irs.gov/businesses/small/article/0,,id=97860,00.html

Text from Web site:

APPLY ONLINE

The Internet EIN application is the preferred method for customers to apply for and obtain an EIN. Once the application is completed, the information is validated during the online session, and an EIN is issued immediately. The online application process is available for all entities whose principal business, office, or agency, or legal residence (in the case of an individual), is located in the United States or U.S. Territories. The principal officer, general partner, grantor, owner, trustor etc. must have a valid Taxpayer Identification Number (Social Security Number, Employer Identification Number, or Individual Taxpayer Identification Number) in order to use the online application.

APPLY BY EIN TOLL-FREE TELEPHONE SERVICE

Taxpayers can obtain an EIN immediately by calling the Business & Specialty Tax Line at (800) 829–4933. The hours of operation are 7:00 a.m.–10:00 p.m. local time, Monday through Friday. An assistor takes the information, assigns the EIN, and provides the number to an authorized individual over the telephone. Note: International applicants must call (215) 516–6999 (Not a toll-free number).

APPLY BY FAX

Taxpayers can FAX the completed Form SS-4 (PDF) application to their state FAX number (see Where to File – Business Forms and Filing Addresses), after ensuring that the Form SS-4 contains all of the required information. If it is determined that the entity needs a new EIN, one will be assigned using the appropriate procedures for the entity type. If the taxpayer's fax number is provided, a fax will be sent back with the EIN within four (4) business days.

APPLY BY MAIL

The processing timeframe for an EIN application received by mail is four weeks. Ensure that the Form SS-4 (PDF) contains all of the required information. If it is determined that the entity needs a new EIN, one will be assigned using the appropriate procedures for the entity type and mailed to the taxpayer.

OTHER IMPORTANT INFORMATION
THIRD-PARTY AUTHORIZATION

The Third Party Designee section must be completed at the bottom of the Form SS-4. The Form SS-4 must also be signed by the taxpayer for the third party designee authorization to be valid. The Form SS-4 must be mailed or faxed to the appropriate service center. A third party designee may call for an EIN; however a faxed Form SS-4, with the taxpayer's signature, is still required. IRS assistors will take the information over the phone from the third party designee and ask the third party to fax the completed Form SS-4 to them (to the IRS assistor's attention) at an administrative fax number. After receiving the faxed Form SS-4, the EIN will be assigned and faxed back to the third party designee, or given over the phone. The third party designee's authority terminates at the time the EIN is assigned and released to the designee.

The EIN is also used to file tax returns for the trust itself. IRS Form 1041 is a trust tax return that must be filed for every year that the trust has income. Often money is held in investments for a period of time before it is passed out to the beneficiaries.

This may be because the trust provides for scheduled distributions to beneficiaries rather than a lump sum, or it may be a trust that is being managed for the lifetime of a beneficiary or group of beneficiaries. The trust must report the income to the IRS, and an EIN is necessary to do that.

DISTRIBUTING THE ASSETS

After all the assets are gathered together and the debts are paid, it is time to distribute the assets left in the trust according to the trust instructions. For most trusts this is merely a matter of writing checks to the heirs in the shares dictated by the trust document. Sometimes, though, all the assets have not been liquidated and money is just sitting in an account waiting, for instance, for the sale of that last piece of real estate. As the trustee, you do not have to wait for every single asset to be converted to cash before you start divvying up the shares.

Partial distributions can be made. The trustee may, for example, hand out 90 percent of the trust assets and hold back 10 percent to cover the final tax return, or to pay expenses on that house that hasn't sold yet, then make a final distribution when everything is complete. The amount of a partial distribution would depend on the expected future expenses.

Get receipts. In the "Forms" section is a Receipt for Distributive Share form. This should be signed by each heir when he or she receives a distribution and kept by the trustee. The form provides protections for the trustee so that there are not complaints later on.

THE TRUST THAT CONTINUES AFTER DEATH

Trusts do not always end as soon as the assets are identified and the debts are paid. Often the trust acts as an asset manager for some or all heirs. Children, disabled heirs, and spendthrifts may find the trustee controlling their trust funds for them for a period of years, until they reach a certain age, or even for their lifetime. How does the trustee set up this sort of trust and manage the funds?

After identifying the assets, paying the bills, giving out the personal things to those who are to get them, and distributing shares to those whose trust share is not going to continue to be held in trust, the next step is to begin following the instructions of the trust grantor to manage assets for the remaining beneficiaries.

1. Get a Tax ID Number for the trust if you have not already done so. How to get one is explained earlier in this chapter.

2. Invest the assets that are to be managed for the trust beneficiary. As a trustee you are required to make safe, conservative investments. The rule generally is the "prudent investor rule," which means you must diversify the investments and not do anything risky that could jeopardize them. My recommendation is to contact an investment advisor, such as one of the large brokerage houses or a certified financial planner, and have that advisor set up a diversified portfolio for the trust, allowing you the ability to access the assets as needed to pay the expenses of the trust beneficiary.

For example, if you are the trustee for a trust for minor children with the provisions that the money may be used for their support, maintenance, education, and medical needs, you will need to be able to direct payments from the trust assets for these purposes. If there is more than one child benefiting from the trust, you would direct the broker to set up separate asset accounts for each child so that each is drawing from his own share of the total. (Some trusts may let everyone draw from the same pot of assets, so there would be only one asset account.)

Typically, the balance of a child's share not used for the permitted purposes would be turned over upon the child reaching a certain age, such as twenty-five. A trust for a disabled person may continue for the person's lifetime but would be invested and managed the same way.

Any trust that continues beyond the death of the grantor becomes a separate legal taxpaying entity. The trustee must file an income tax return for the trust every year just as if the trust were a real person or a company.

The trust must come to an end at some point. Most states have a law called the "rule against perpetuities." This law means that a trust may not be perpetual and that at some point all the trust assets have to be given to someone. This rule is flexible, since the typical one allows a trust to stay in place for "a life in being plus twenty-one years." So if you had two children and two grandchildren and wanted to set up a trust that provided the income to your children for life, then their children for their lifetimes, then to your great grandchildren for twenty-one years, the trust could stay in existence for that long without violating the rule.

The rule against perpetuities does not in all states apply to all assets that may be placed in trust, nor is it a rule everywhere. It may only apply to real estate, for example, when a person wants to keep the cottage in the family. Check with your lawyer if you want to set up this type of trust provision or if you are the trustee of a trust with the provision in it.

APPENDIX A

Forms and Form Letters

The following form letters and forms are provided for educational purposes and are not intended to act as legal advice. While these work for most areas, I cannot guarantee what particular rules and laws may require different things where you live. Often organizations will respond to a form letter by sending you their own forms to fill out, so these may act to help initiate the process rather than completing it. Before relying on these, be sure to get the advice of an attorney in your area.

The addresses were current at press time, but should be checked. These letters may be too small to photocopy, but retyping is easy enough.

1. Notice to Creditors: Decedent's Trust Estate. (This is published once in the local newspaper where the deceased lived. In some states, publishing this notice creates a short statute of limitations for potential or unknown creditors. Ask your attorney

about the legal efficacy of this form in the jurisdiction of the deceased.)

2. Funeral and Burial Arrangements. (You, as the grantor, should fill out this form for the use of your trustee so that your wishes are known and any prepaid items are revealed to the family.)

3. Obituary. (This is a matter of personal preference and local custom. Often funeral homes will have formats, but this gives you a place to start.)

4. Letter to Life Insurance Company.

5. Letter to Social Security.

6. Letter to Health Insurance Company.

7. Letter to Veteran's Administration.

8. Letter to Organization. (Often membership organizations have group benefit programs that may offer death benefits or services to the family.)

9. Letter to Civil Service Commission.

10. Letter to Employer.

11. Receipt for Distributive Share. (To be signed by any beneficiary and retained by the trustee as a receipt when the trustee distributes assets.)

NOTICE TO CREDITORS
DECEDENT'S TRUST ESTATE

TRUST ESTATE OF   _____
                       (name of deceased)

To all creditors:

NOTICE TO CREDITORS: The decedent, _____
                                       (name of deceased)

who lived at

_____ ,

(address of deceased)

died on _____ 20 _____ .

Creditors of the decedent are notified that all claims against the trust estate will be forever barred unless presented to _____ , the successor trustee named in The _____ Revocable
                               (name of deceased)
Living Trust established by decedent on the _____
day of _____ , 20_____.
All such claims must be presented to the said successor trustee within 4 months after the date of publication of this notice.

_____   _____

Date   Trustee Name

                            _____

                            Address

                            _____

                            Telephone

PUBLISH ABOVE INFORMATION ONLY

Publish one time in _____
                            Name of Newspaper

Furnish Affidavit of Publication and statement of publication charges to the trustee whose address is above.

FUNERAL AND BURIAL ARRANGEMENTS

Prepaid items and location, also include location of supporting paperwork:

Item Location _____

Cemetery Lot _____

Headstone _____

Funeral Services/Supplies _____

Persons or Organizations to notify (including Veterans Administration and organizations such as Masons who you may want to be involved in the funeral ceremony. You may want to attach a list of other people with contact information if these are not known by your family.)

_____

_____

_____

_____

Church or religious organization to which you belong

_____

Who would you like to officiate at a funeral ceremony?

_____

Specific burial instructions (such as whether or not you want cremation or where you would like to be buried)

_____

Cemetery plot location (or desired location to purchase a plot)

_____

Deed to plot location if any is located

_____

Church/synagogue to notify

_____

Date _____ Your Signature _____

OBITUARY

An obituary has several standard formats, varying by region of the country, religious orientation, and family tradition. Most newspapers will print whatever you decide to write. Some papers run these for free, while others charge you based on how long the obituary is and how many days it is to run.

Here is the traditional simplified format, though this can run longer or even shorter.

> John William Jones, age 89, died Saturday, March 12, in Ann Arbor, Michigan.
> Services will be held at the Moore Funeral Home on March 16 at 2:00 PM followed by burial at Sunset Gardens Park where a graveside service will be held.
> John was a member of Westside Church and retired from Ford Motor Company. He is survived by his wife Barbara and his two children Nathan and Kristine.
>
> Memorial contributions may be made to the National Heart Fund.

LETTER TO LIFE INSURANCE COMPANY

Date _____

Name and Address of Insurance Company

Dear Sir or Madam:

Re: _____
    Insert Name of Deceased

Date of Death _____

The above named person had a policy with your company.

Policy Number _____

Please send me information on the death benefits or accrued benefits during the lifetime of the deceased and all claim forms needed to claim these benefits.

Please let me know what other information or documents you may need me to provide.

_____

Your Signature

_____

Print Name
Your Address
Your Telephone and E-mail

LETTER TO SOCIAL SECURITY

Date _____

Social Security Administration
Address of Local Social Security Office

Dear Sir or Madam:

Re: _____
    Insert Name of Deceased

Date of Death _____

Social Security Number _____

I am writing to inform you of the death of the above person. A copy of the death certificate is enclosed. I would like to arrange a meeting to discuss the options and benefits available to the surviving spouse and/or family.

Please either call me or let me know how to proceed to set up such a meeting.

Thank you for your help.

_____

Your Signature

_____

Print Name
Your Address
Your Telephone and E-mail

LETTER TO HEALTH INSURANCE COMPANY

Date _____

Name and Address of Insurance Company

Dear Sir or Madam:

Re: _____
    Insert Name of Deceased

Date of Death _____

The above named person had a policy with your company.

Policy Number _____

Please send me information on the death benefits or accrued benefits during the lifetime of the deceased and all claim forms needed to claim these benefits.

Please let me know what other information or documents you may need me to provide.

_____

Your Signature

_____

Print Name
Your Address
Your Telephone and E-mail

LETTER TO VETERAN'S ADMINISTRATION

Date _____

Veteran's Administration
Insurance Division
500 Wissachickon Avenue   or   Fort Snelling
Philadelphia, PA 19010   St. Paul, MN 55111

Re: _____
    Insert Name of Deceased

Date of Death _____

Dear Sir or Madam:

I represent the estate of the above named person whose Social
Security Number is _____ .

I have enclosed a photocopy of the death certificate.

He may have had insurance or other benefits due to him; please let
me know what was available and the forms or procedures to claim
those benefits.

The information I have is as follows:

Branch of Service _____

Date of Entering Service _____

Discharge Date _____

Service Number (if different than Social Security Number)

_____

Please let me know what other information or documents you may
need me to provide.

_____

Your Signature

_____

Print Name
Your Address
Your Telephone and E-mail

LETTER TO ORGANIZATION

Date _____

Name and Address of Organization

Re: _____
 Insert Name of Deceased

Date of Death _____

Dear Sir or Madam:

I represent the estate of the above named person whose Social
Security Number is _____ .

I have enclosed a photocopy of the death certificate.

Please let me know what benefits may be available to the deceased
and/or his family, including such things as life insurance, disability, vacation and sick pay, retirement, or other benefits. If there are
claim forms for these please send them to me or let me know how
to get them.

Please let me know what other information or documents you may
need.

Sincerely,

_____

Your Signature

_____

Print Name
Your Address
Your Telephone and E-mail

LETTER TO CIVIL SERVICE COMMISSION

(Date) _____

Civil Service Commission
1900 East Street, N.W.
Washington, D.C. 20415

Re: _____
    Insert Name of Deceased

Date of Death _____

Dear Sir or Madam:

I represent the estate of the above named person whose Social Security Number is _____ .

I have enclosed a photocopy of the death certificate.

Please let me know what benefits may be available to the deceased and/or his family, including such things as life insurance, disability, vacation and sick pay, retirement, or other benefits. If there are claim forms for these please send them to me or let me know how to get them.

Please let me know what other information or documents you may need.

Sincerely,

_____
Your Signature

_____
Print Name
Your Address
Your Telephone and E-maill

LETTER TO EMPLOYER

(Date) _____

Name of Employer _____
Address _____
_____

Dear Sir or Madam:

I represent the estate of your employee/former employee whose name is _____ and whose Social Security Number is _____ .

Please let me know if there are any accrued and unpaid benefits available to him or payable to his estate. This might include unpaid vacation or sick pay, group life insurance, pension or retirement benefits, stock options or stock purchase plans, profit sharing, disability income, payroll savings, or any other benefits. If the deceased left personal property in your possession, please let me know how to arrange for pickup.

Also, if there are claim forms available to access these benefits, could you please forward those or tell me how to get them.

I have enclosed a photocopy of the death certificate.

Please let me know what other information or documents you may need.

Sincerely,

_____

Your Signature

_____

Print Name
Your Address
Your Telephone and E-mail

RECEIPT FOR DISTRIBUTIVE SHARE

I hereby acknowledge the receipt of the following asset(s) from the following trust estate:

_____ :

Name and Date of Trust

Description of asset(s) received:

This is a _____ full or _____ partial distribution to me from the estate.

I acknowledge that I have received a copy of the trust document as well as an accounting of trust assets and expenditures to date and am satisfied with the same.

Dated: _____

_____
Signature

_____
Print Name

Short Form:
Guide to Trust Funding

See the information in this book for detailed instructions and letters of instruction for various types of assets. This list covers most things for most people.

Below are some guidelines on transferring some kinds of property to a trust. If you have property not listed below, contact the institution in charge of it and ask about their procedure or look in the detailed instructions. Keep in mind that each company you deal with will have its own procedure, forms, and preferred language they use when making transfers to your trust, so be prepared to be flexible. They will want to see your certificate of trust existence or the trust itself. It is okay to give them a copy, but under no circumstances let them keep the original.

In general, transfers of assets to the trust will be done as follows:

1. Transfer directly into the name of the trust. The assets (such as real estate, bank accounts, CDs, money markets, and stocks) will be in the name of your trust rather than in your name. You will contact the institution and request this change (using, for example, the General Account Transfer Letter in your packet) and the institution will change the ownership of the account or asset to the name of the trust.

2. Life insurance is changed by changing the primary beneficiary to the name of the trust if you want it to be part of the trust assets.

3. Tax deferred assets, such as IRAs, 401(k)s, TIAA-CREF, 403(b)s, etc., depend upon several things. If you are married, the spouse normally remains the primary beneficiary in order to retain all roll-over elections in an easy manner. The trust would be the second or alternate beneficiary if you want these assets controlled by the trust; otherwise you can directly name the second beneficiary and leave these out of the trust. Typically if you have children, you will want the trust as the second beneficiary rather than the children. A single person will either name the trust as primary beneficiary or an individual person. You can discuss this with your attorney or financial advisor. Payout elections may still be available to beneficiaries if the trust provisions are complete using the "look-through" provisions of the IRS code.

4. Certain credit union and bank accounts, brokerage accounts—particularly those with direct deposit—pension and Social Security accounts, may be more

easily handled by a "pay on death" (POD) or "transfer on death" (TOD) designation. A transfer form is included herein for that purpose. (Credit unions sometimes require this procedure since some do not allow trusts to own accounts.)

5. Automobiles, motorcycles, boats, trailers, and other things with titles can be put into the trust name at the Secretary of State's office or tax office—whatever it is called in your jurisdiction—if there are no liens on the titles. Sometimes there is an alternate way to transfer titles. If there is to be no probate—and there would not be with a fully funded trust—the state may transfer titles to the next of kin merely by seeing the death certificate and signing their affidavit.

Personal property such as furniture and household goods, jewelry, collections, animals, tools, farm equipment, or other tangible assets without titles will be part of the trust by virtue of the Assignment of Assets form, which is part of every well-written trust.

APPENDIX C

Estate and Capital Gains Taxes

At the time of this writing, the federal estate tax laws are in a state of flux and are likely to change due to pending legislation and the phasing out of the 2001 Tax Reconciliation Act. I do not want to make this too complicated, because detailed tax issues are beyond the scope and intent of this book. However, if the law stands as it is now, expensive consequences could result for a lot of estates for those who die after December 31, 2009.

On January 1, 2010, the Federal Estate Tax is repealed. On January 1, 2011, it is scheduled to be reinstated with a threshold of $1 million. It is very likely that the law will be changed to reinstate the tax with a threshold of $3.5 million, which was the threshold in 2009. If it is not, those who are married with taxable estates exceeding $1 million need to be sure their trust contains provisions allowing a preservation of the exemption of the first spouse to die to effectively double the exemption amount to $2 million.

Remember that the taxable estate means nearly all assets as far as the IRS is concerned, including such things as the death benefit from life insurance, real estate, retirement accounts (such as IRAs, 401(k)s, 403(b)s, and many other kinds), bank deposit accounts, stock portfolios, personal property, business interests—basically all of the things a person owns or that come into being at her death. It is not hard to exceed a $1 million threshold.

If the threshold is increased, this will not be an issue for most folks. However, there is another area of the law that may be even more costly than the Federal Estate Tax, and which may affect even more people.

CAPITAL GAINS TAX

The Capital Gains Tax is a tax on the profit made from selling an asset. The profit is the difference between what you paid for it and the sale price. So if you bought $100 worth of stock and sold it for $500, the $400 profit is your capital gain. The gain is taxed on your tax return at a capital gain tax rate, which changes from time to time as part of various tax reform measures but may be from 15 to 25 percent. The price you paid is called your *tax basis*.

Under the law before January 1, 2010, if you had an asset that had gone up in value, then you died and someone inherited the asset, the person inheriting it received what is called a *stepped-up tax basis*. This means that the new owner had a tax basis that increased to the value as of the date of death, or $500. So if the stock was sold for $500 or less, there would be no taxable profit because the tax basis was increased.

This stepped-up basis will expire on January 1, 2010 unless the law changes. What this means to you is that instead of getting a stepped-up basis, your heirs now get what is called a *carry-over tax basis*. So the heir inherits the stock, sells it for $500, and has a taxable gain of $400. This may not seem so significant, but suppose we are talking about Mom and Dad's house that they paid $75,000 for thirty years ago, which is now worth $375,000? Now there is a $300,000 gain, which could have a $75,000 tax owed on its sale! This carryover basis also applies when a lifetime gift of an asset is made. One of the reasons to have an asset go through an estate rather than be given to a person during lifetime has been to obtain the step-up basis rather than carryover basis. This advantage may no longer exist.

There are provisions proposed that are supposed to ameliorate the new rule for some people. One is that the executor of an estate (and presumably the trustee of a trust) can select assets worth a total of $1.3 million to get the stepped-up basis. (Plus, if the heir is a surviving spouse, an additional $3 million.) But there are stringent reporting requirements to the IRS, which if not followed can result in expensive penalties. Also, the rules require that all records relating to the carryover basis be available, meaning that, for real estate, any improvements made that can increase the tax basis have to have documentary proof. This may mean keeping records for generations for property that may not be sold immediately.

I am recommending specific instructions to the successor trustee regarding this rule, if it is not revoked, and a provision in the trust document directing how the stepped-up basis is to be allocated if total assets exceed the $1.3 million limit.

The net result of the rule is that even if the Federal Estate Tax is totally eliminated, the new capital gains rules will actually bring in more money to the Treasury and hit more people of modest means than did the estate tax. The Joint Committee on Taxation estimated that eliminating the estate tax would cost the government $281 billion in the first five years, but they would gain $293 billion in new revenue from the capital gains change for a net increase of $12 billion. But what is likely to happen is not elimination of the estate tax, just an increase in the threshold—so this is a big new tax increase unless it is changed.

Glossary of Terms

Beneficiary: In a trust, the person who benefits from the trust assets. Initially the beneficiary will be the grantor, then at the death of the grantor the benficiaries are the people or organizations named in the trust who are to receive the trust assets. *Heir* is sometimes used to mean beneficiary.

Conservator: A person appointed by a court to be the financial manager of the assets of a minor or an incapacitated or incompetent adult.

Employer Identification Number: A number issued by the IRS to use as the taxpayer number for the trust. This is like a Social Security Number for a person.

Estate and Inheritance Taxes: Taxes paid to the state or federal government based upon a percentage of the total taxable estate of a deceased person. Typically no taxes are due unless the total estate size exceeds a preset threshold amount.

Fiduciary: A person who is in a special position of trust regarding the financial affairs of another.

Funding: The process of transferring assets to a trust.

Grantor: The person who creates the trust is the grantor. Also sometimes called the *settlor* or *trustor*.

Guardian: A person appointed by a court to care for a minor or a legally disabled adult. The guardian cares for the person while the conservator cares for the person's financial affairs.

Heir: A person who inherits property from a person who dies whether through a will, a trust, or a beneficiary designation. Also commonly called a *beneficiary*.

Intestate: A person who dies without a will is said to have died intestate, whereas one who dies with a will is said to have died testate. Think last will and *testament*.

Issue: The direct blood-related descendants of a person, i.e., children, grandchildren, great grandchildren.

Joint Tenancy: A co-ownership of property by two or more parties in which each party owns an undivided interest that passes to the other co-owners on her death (known as the "right of survivorship").

Life Tenant: A person who has the right to the use of certain property for his lifetime. For real estate, this right is sometimes called a life lease or a life estate.

Living Trust: A written document that, when signed and funded properly, becomes a legal entity that has the ability to control the assets it owns and states who will receive those assets under certain conditions as well as who is in charge of seeing that these instructions are carried out. (Simply, who gets what, when they get it, and who is in charge of seeing that that happens.)

Patient Advocate: The person who acts under a medical power of attorney to make medical decisions for a person who is unable to make those decisions for herself. This is done by appointment in a medical power of attorney.

Personal Representative: This is the person who is in charge of the probate of an estate. Sometimes called an executor where there is a will, or an administrator where there is no will.

Power of Attorney: A document that gives a person (an agent, sometimes called an attorney-in-fact) the legal right to transact the business of another person (the principal). This permission to sign is limited to the exact rights set out in the document as though the original principal had signed himself. Sometimes called a proxy. A durable power of attorney is one that is still valid even if the principal becomes incapacitated. A springing power of attorney is one that becomes effective only upon the happening of a certain event, such as a person becoming incapacitated (a person could have a springing durable power of attorney). A power of attorney is valid until it is revoked or the principal dies.

Probate: A legal court process through which assets in the name of the deceased person are transferred to those who are entitled to them after paying all debts of the deceased and the expenses of administering the probate case. Probate may be used to settle disputes as to the validity of a will, trust, or other document. The probate court has authority over all issues relating to the financial affairs of deceased persons. Separate sections of the probate court may involve the affairs of minors, juvenile offenses, guardianships, conservatorships, and handicapped adults.

Revocable Living Trust: A living trust in which terms may be amended, modified, or otherwise revoked by the grantor during her lifetime, as opposed to an irrevocable trust, which may not be changed once created. A revocable trust typically becomes an irrevocable trust at the death or incapacity of the grantor.

Rule Against Perpetuities: A state law determining how long a trust may stay in existence.

Special-Needs Trust: A trust that manages assets for a beneficiary who may be unable to manage his own financial affairs, typically to pay for living expenses beyond those provided by agencies and programs such as Medicaid and set things up so that the beneficiary is not disqualified from those aid plans.

Successor Trustee: The person who is in charge of the trust assets at the death or incapacity of the grantor. If the grantor is incapacitated mentally or physically so as to be unable to manage the trust, the successor trustee manages the grantor's business affairs during that time. At the grantor's death, the successor trustee is responsible for carrying out the grantor's instructions as written in the trust for the distribution of the trust assets, as well as taking care of any tax issues for the estate.

Tenants in Common: Where two or more people own property jointly but each has separate ownership of her share without a right of survivorship with the other co-owners. A tenant in common may transfer her separate share of an asset without the permission of the other owners in most cases.

Testator: A person who makes a will. If the person is female, a testatrix. Archaic language.

Trustee: The person who is in charge of the trust assets and who carries out the instructions in the trust. Normally the grantor is the trustee during his lifetime. At the grantor's death or incapacity, the successor trustee takes over.

Trust Protector: A person (or group of people) appointed in a trust document to oversee the trustee. This person sometimes has the power to modify the terms of the trust herself.

Index

Books from Allworth Press

Allworth Press is an imprint of Allworth Communications, Inc. Selected titles are listed below.

Your Living Trust and Estate Plan, 3rd Edition
by Harvey J. Platt (6 × 9, 320 pages, paperback, $16.95)

Estate Planning and Administration: How to Maximize Assets and Protect Loved Ones
by Edmund T. Fleming (6 × 9, 192 pages, paperback, $16.95)

Estate Planning for the Healthy Wealthy Family
by Stanley D. Neeleman, Carla B. Garrity, and Mitchell A. Barris (6 × 9, 256 pages, paperback, $22.95)

Legal Forms for Everyone
by Carl W. Battle (8 1/2 × 11, 240 pages, paperback, includes CD-ROM, $24.95)

Winning the Divorce War: How to Protect Your Best Interests, 2nd Edition
by Ronald Sharp (5 1/2 × 8 1/2, 208 pages, paperback, $16.95)

Feng Shui and Money: A Nine-Week Program for Creating Wealth Using Ancient Principles and Techniques
By Eric J. Shaffert (6 × 9, 256 pages, paperback, $16.95)

The Money Mentor: A Tale of Finding Financial Freedom
by Tad Crawford (6 × 9, 272 pages, paperback, $24.95)

Turn Your Idea or Invention into Millions
by Don Kracke (6 × 9, 224 pages, paperback, $18.95)

Spend Your Way to Wealth
By Mike Schiano (6 × 9, 208 pages, paperback, $21.95)

How to Escape Lifetime Security and Pursue Your Impossible Dream: A Guide to Transforming Your Career
by Kenneth Atchity (5 1/2 × 8 1/2, 208 pages, paperback, $16.95)

Old Money: The Mythology of Wealth in America (Expanded Edition)
by Nelson W. Aldrich, Jr. (6 × 9, 340 pages, paperback, $24.95)

The Secret Life of Money: How Money Can Be Food for the Soul
by Tad Crawford (5 1/2 × 8 1/2, 304 pages, paperback, $19.95)

To request a free catalog or order books by credit card, call 1-800-491-2808. To see our complete catalog on the World Wide Web, or to order online, please visit **www.allworth.com**.